# THE
# COMMUNITY PLAYHOUSE

*A Manual on Its Organization and Maintenance*

BY

## C. J. DE GOVEIA

39389

NEW YORK  B. W. HUEBSCH, Inc. MCMXXIII

# PREFACE

This book is for the beginner in Community Playhouse art. It makes no bid for the field of the advanced worker. Theoretical and controversial questions have been left out for the most part, the author's purpose being, whenever possible, to give definite facts, figures and examples. In talks with groups in various parts of the country in the process of organization, the author has met invariably with the request: "Give us something definite to work on; there is nothing published, and the little theatre speakers we've had dealt only in theories and generalities. We don't care so much about what Gordon Craig did in Italy as about what we can do here at home."

It is true that many art theatre representatives, either from their attempt to prove themselves thoroughly familiar with their subject, or from their failure to establish any contact with the beginner, merely mystify or discourage their audiences with technical discourses. Most of the books now published on this subject suffer from these objects.

It is to help those people who need a practical guide that this book is written. No attempt has been made to be exhaustive. The book has been made purposely short. Chapters on "Color," "Grouping," and "Lighting," have been introduced merely to call the reader's attention to the fact that these are elements with which the worker must deal.

The author wishes to thank those who have contributed diagrams and information concerning their theatres, and to acknowledge his obligations to Messrs. Henry Holt & Co., D. Appleton & Co., B. W. Huebsch, Little, Brown & Co., and the Yale University Press for use of material published by them. Especially for helpful suggestions and co-operation does he wish to thank Elson Barnes Norbury and Clarence Gray.

# TABLE OF CONTENTS

# TABLE OF CONTENTS

# THE COMMUNITY PLAYHOUSE

## I

## INTRODUCTORY

BEFORE the promoter attempts to establish a Community Playhouse in his village or city, it is imperative that he understand clearly just what such an institution is.  Surely this is not too much to demand even of the most unseasoned tyro.

Yet many Community Playhouses have been started in recent years by promoters who have been quite in the dark over what it was all about, and have been spurred on only, it would seem, by the apparently universal impulse to express themselves. The failure in this country after a season or two, or even at the outset, of so many of these little theatres has been due, in a majority of cases, either to lack of definite knowledge on the part of the members of what the organization has set out to do, to the manner in which the attempt has been made, or to insufficient consideration of the possible audience.

In my intercourse with votaries of the Community Playhouse movement in various parts of the country, I have found that there exists a general haziness about the entire subject. There seems to be a lack of exact knowledge about purpose, organization, production. Especially is this true in the Middle Western and Southern cities. Certain art lovers are seized with the idea of establishing a Community Playhouse in their town for social, educational or play reasons and with little or no preparation set out to put that idea into effect. They probably have read an article or two in periodicals about the work of the Provincetown Players in their delightful little work-shop, or of the accomplishments of the Neighborhood Playhouse; perhaps they have seen a performance of the Wisconsin Players or the Community Theatre at Hollywood, and at once conclude that their city is sorely in need of such an institution. They are right in this; for no city in the United States of a population of two thousand or more should be without its Community Playhouse.

But it is essential that those who attempt to establish these theatres should have some knowledge of what they are undertaking. Many permanent theatres have been kept back for years by abortive attempts of impulsive individuals to sow seed on untilled soil.

The kind of city in which the promoter lives will determine the kind of little theatre which he must start.

Boston and Peoria, Illinois, have little in common. The population of one is largely art-loving; that of the other, commercial. Nor would one expect the same kind of organization in New York City as in Milwaukee. This is not so much on account of the size of the various cities; it is a matter rather of the kind of people living in them. The atmosphere of New York is imperialistic, that of Galesburg, Illinois, democratic. The Washington Square Players, several years ago, succeeded on the imperialistic business principles of the commercial stage; Crafton's Prairie Playhouse grew and lived because it belonged to the people and was, indeed, a growth of their own art.

Nothing is more absurd than to suppose that the

desire of two enthusiasts is a sufficient basis for the establishment of a Community Playhouse—unless indeed these two persons have an annual income on which to live and an investment fund to sink.[1] Even in this case success of the project would be doubtful, although there is a chance that the tastes of the two enthusiasts might coincide with that of the audience supposed to support them.  If this happens, other things being equal, the theatre may well prosper.

But it is useless for a group of players to try to change the taste of an entire community.  Those who have an inherent desire for vaudeville will patronize vaudeville houses in spite of all the art that goes ragged in the Little Theatres.  They may be induced to attend a performance or two of something different, but they will eventually drift back to their slapstick and broad comedy.

Many attempts have been made in this country by aspiring groups to promote theatres of the municipal, repertory, social and art types.  Most of these

[1] See Dickinson's "The Insurgent Theatre" and Burton's "The Community Theatre" for the advocacy of that idea.

attempts, for various reasons, have been unsuccess-
ful. The municipal theatre of Northampton,
Mass., in spite of excellent financial and civic
support lasted but three seasons; the Chicago Little
Theatre, the best of the Art Theatre type, scarcely
weathered two, and the New Theatre of New York
City, a repertory theatre built on colossal lines,
little more than made a start.

The Community Playhouse is none of these types
individually, but it may, and often does, take on
some of the qualities of each of them. The federated audience, civic interest, the choosing of liberal
programs, the keeping intact of the players' group
are a few of the parts where the borderline is indis-
tinct. Indeed, the distinction lies more in purpose
than in form.

# II

## THE COMMUNITY PLAYHOUSE

As yet, in the United States, there is no perfect example of the Community Playhouse in the strictest sense of the term. There are several groups, however, working toward that end. This is especially true in the provincial districts and in cities of the Middle West. The Little County Theatre, Fargo, N. D., is progressing rapidly toward this goal; the Richmond Hill Players of Richmond Hill, Long Island, New York, are perfecting their organization to include the community, and the Wisconsin Players are broadening their influence every year.

In the South the Little Theatre of New Orleans, in the West, the Community Theatre of Hollywood and the Denver Players at Denver, in the Middle West, the Cleveland Players, are a few of the organizations which are annually branching out with community influence. The demise of the Arts and

Crafts Theatre in Detroit, some seasons ago, removed from the field a group of players who were destined to make an impression on American dramatic art.

The Neighborhood Playhouse of New York City and the Provincetown Players continue to dominate the Eastern field, while with each season the 47 Workshop of George Baker at Harvard adds to its effective work.

The author prefers to use the term Community Playhouse as applying to those little theatres which, through community coöperation, are able to provide their own dramatic amusement. This does not mean that the plays must be written by local dramatists, though they often are; it does not mean that these local plays must be woven around local people, although good work has been done along that line. It signifies rather an institution which provides the means whereby a community, or a class of people large enough to support it, can give individual expression to their dramatic impulses, learn the technique of the stage, and support the best plays of the type which appeals to them.

While the Community Playhouse may have various meanings and purposes, social, educational, artistic, recreational or whatnot, its organization falls naturally into three elements—*Players' Group*, *Audience* and *Building*. Each is equally important. Each fills a definite purpose.

*The Players' Group* usually is made up of local talent. Writers who have something to say to a public; actors who are learning their profession, or professionals who use this means to create; producers who have ability and want to express it; artists who want to work out, unhampered, ideas of stage setting and designing; mechanics, electricians and carpenters—are among those who make up the group. They may be professional, semi-professional or amateurs; they may work for profit or experience. That does not matter. They have affiliated themselves with the players' group for some reason of play.

*The Audience*, the second element of the Community Playhouse organization, may be one of several kinds. It will probably be a composite. Lovers of good drama, people who have a desire for something better than the "movies" or the cheap commercial shows which come to their town; "high-brows" who attend for the sole purpose of being bored; society folk who go to be amused and to see their friends; Puritans of the straight-back variety who go to be shocked, are the classes who make up an audience.   The audience of a Community Play-house is usually made up of all these with some one element dominating.   The dominant element decides the type which the theatre is to be and often-times the length of its life as well.

In most Little Theatres, the audience is fed-erated.   That is, a certain number of people in the community agree to stand behind the players to the extent of a fixed number of tickets for a season. These persons are sometimes called patrons, sup-porting members, or contributing members.

The average audience supporting Community Playhouses is approximately 400 members.

*The Building* is the last element of the Commu-nity Playhouse.   It is by no means the least impor-tant.   A survey of the players' groups of the country reveals the fact that only groups which have permanent homes endure the stress of time.

The kind of building depends on the location of the group, finances and resourcefulness.   It is their home.   In this building their work is presented to the public, rehearsals are carried on and experiments made.   It is the instrument whereby their art may be given a hearing.   Around it cling memories of successes and failures and it becomes more important as each season goes by.

The *Players' Group*, the *Audience* and the *Building* will be taken up at more length in the following three chapters.

# III

## THE PLAYERS' GROUP

You who are reading these chapters will probably be the promoter, or at least one of the promoters, of a Community Playhouse in your city. It will fall to you to take the first step toward organization. That first step is a study of the material for the players' group.

Who will be in it?

Doubtless the first thought is: Who can act? But acting is only a part of an artistic production.

In "Some Reasons for Being" one players' group announced in its prospectus: "We intend to establish an experimental stage for the use of actors, writers, painters and musicians who wish to participate in developing art in the theatre."

A players' group, therefore, is not made up entirely of actors.

Setting aside, for the present, the audience, of whom you must be able to count upon at least 250, your players' group should contain as a minimum:

Six men and five women members with acting ability.
One director.
One business executive.
One artist.
One designer.
One electrician.
One dance instructor.
Several persons handy with carpenter's tools.
As many more as are needed to fill committees on costume, play-choosing, play-reading, membership, etc.

The players' group should contain not less than twenty members and not more than fifty. Larger groups are unwieldy.

The promoter, before setting out, should have an intelligent idea as to who should constitute the group. If he does not, he has little business promoting a Community Playhouse. The chief stumbling-block, however, is to draw his elements together and direct the line of accomplishment.

Some playhouses are run on a strictly society

basis; others, by a group of artists as a means of expression, and still others as a community venture. I know of no Little Theatre in which the three elements have been successfully mixed. Just before the recent war, we had planned in Peoria, Illinois, to establish several playhouses in industrial centres of the city, another made up of people interested in art, and still another for the so-called society group. Individual directors were to be in charge of each of these playhouses, with a central board controlling them all. This central board was to have been directed by a director-generalissimo. The best players and craftsmen of the individual playhouses were to have been brought up to the main playhouse as they demonstrated their ability. In this way the entire city was to have been covered. Inasmuch as this plan, owing to the war, was never completed, its workableness has never been given a trial.

First of all, then, you must decide upon the type of group you wish to form. However you may set to work—whether you call a general meeting of those interested or hold a public try-out, one thing is absolutely clear—definite plans must be presented at the first assembly of prospective members. This is imperative.

When you have convened the meeting, talk over the matter of the Community Playhouse—just what you intend to do, your aims and ambitions. If possible, secure a speaker from some established players' group. An outside influence, if it is enthusiastic, is a decided stimulus.

Of course, it will be impossible for you to outline the full program of plays to be given during the season, or to choose your casts or erect your building or consider the thousand and one other details that will arise during the course of production. But a general outline of the season's work, the type of plays to be given, the methods of finance, and the personnel of the group—all these questions should be considered before the first meeting.

Suggestions from directors and members of other playhouses are often helpful and sometimes save the beginning group many pitfalls.

There is nothing so detrimental to a new players' group as an enthusiastic aimlessness. Before this first meeting it is absolutely imperative that the promoters should get together and work out exact plans for the organization. Under no circumstances should they meet their prospective supporters with any haziness in their own minds. I am dictatorial in this matter because I have seen so many well-intentioned persons destroy the possibilities of a Community Playhouse by tangential ideas and the lack of definite plans at the first meeting.

Of course I do not mean that the promoter should arbitrarily outline his own plans and attempt to force them through at all hazards. That would be foolhardy and probably disastrous to the whole project. I mean simply that a thorough study of the whole field should be made by the promoting group, and that the latter, on the basis of this knowledge, should have some definite scheme to propose.

There are, of course, other methods of getting the players together. An even more democratic way is to announce through the press that try-outs for a players' group are to be held on a certain date. Several playhouses have been organized in this way. Usually, however, when this method is used, some such organization as a club or a society, or perhaps even some individual, is behind the scheme. It is an excellent idea to have a club or society as sponsor for a players' group, provided that this club or society does not obtrude itself or attempt to force the group into the mold of a class. This is a danger and must be watched by promoters.

Some of the most successful Community Playhouses are organized in the regular club manner: that is, with a constitution which provides for a president, one or more vice-presidents, a secretary, a treasurer and committees. No distinction is made between the audience and the players' group; those who work in the group are called Active Members, while those who are inactive and make up the audience to a large extent are called Associative Members. In such cases the organization is little more than a club, and members of the group and members of the audience are apt to look upon the project in this light. The organization of the Arts and Crafts Theatre in Detroit is much to be preferred. There the players' group and the audience were entirely separate, but the audience or subscribers were represented in the management by an advisory board.

The players' group itself should be organized in the manner of a club. This is the only way in which amateurs can be controlled. On the commercial stage, the director rules with a rod of fines; the unfortunate director of amateurs has only a constitution to refer to. A constitutional organization with elected officers provides the best system for handling a group. The authority of the director is somewhat curtailed, but this is beneficial; for it relieves him, especially in matter of detail, of much responsibility.

At the head of your group will be the *President*. He need not be a man of dramatic ability, although he must be truly interested in the stage and have some knowledge of its workings. He must, however, be an executive, a man of vision, diplomatic and with a reservoir of good common sense. He must be able to meet people of all classes, handle all situations that arise in the group and the audience, and be able to assume with dignity the position of buffer.

Then there will be a *Vice-President*, who will in time succeed the president. While waiting for that position, however, he will be kept busy learning the ropes.    He likewise will be chosen for his qualifications for future office.

The *Secretary* will carry on the usual work of that office, and will usually act as a private secretary to the president and to the director.

The *Treasurer's* duties are manifest.

And now come two offices on the filling of which will probably depend the success or failure of the theatre.

Many groups have started out with the *Director* at the head of everything.    He has read plays, collected money, trained the players, designed the scenes, managed the business end; in fact the director has been the entire organization and has done nine-tenths of the work.    Most of those groups have discovered that this is a mistake.

The choosing of the director is one of the important steps in a group's existence.    Not that it is necessary that the choice should be an individual of wide fame, years of experience, or a marked genius. These qualifications are excellent, but few directors of that type are available.    Certainly he must have some experience.   He must be enthusiastic, he must have vision, directing talent, knowledge of the new methods of staging as well as the old.   He must have a fine discrimination for acting values, he must understand grouping and the building up of stage pictures, and he must possess other qualifications for producing.   Upon him falls the duty of production and he must be sufficiently prepared.   Consequently, he will not be elected by vote of the group as are the other officers.   The type of individuals who make successful directors are usually not popular.   They are considered "queer" people, temperamental and unsocial.

The director will be appointed by the *Executive Board* of the group which is made up of the president, the vice-president, the secretary and the treasurer for this election.   At all other times the director is a member of the board.

The work of the director is clear.   He will have full charge of production.   Under him will be a corps of assistants, either appointed by him, or by the president after consultation with him.   He will be provided with an *Assistant-Director* or *Stage-*

*Manager*, an *Art-Director* and a host of committees who are directly responsible to him.   He is
generalissimo of production just as a coach is of
athletics.   His word is final.

The choosing of a director will depend, of course,
somewhat upon the kind of theatre the community
intends to support.   One requisite, however, is absolutely necessary; to put it rawly, he must have
good common sense.   I have no sympathy—and the
history of the successful Little Theatres in this
country bears me out in this—with the so-called
faddist type of director.   In every new movement
there are always certain individuals who rush in and
try to startle the public by giving them a new kind
of "art."   Whether they are sincere or merely pos-
ing matters little.   The point is, such groups and
individuals keep back saner projects through their
failures and lead to disgust and disillusionment with
the whole idea of community enterprises.

The director who will not meet his audience half-
way, who, in spite of the fact that his public is
made up of commonplace people, attempts to force

down their unwilling throats his favorite ideas is doomed to failure before he begins. It is well and good to keep ahead of the commercial theatre in the class of plays produced, but never so far that the audience supporting the project will lose its interest.

Therein lies the effectiveness of a check upon the director. To be sure, he will have absolute control of production after the play is chosen; but the play itself should be chosen only by a committee who knows its audience and knows them well. Once the play is chosen, however, the director must be given a free hand, and under no circumstances should any committee or individual attempt to interfere with him.

The other important officer is the *Business Manager*. For this position an alert, hustling individual must be secured. Upon him or her falls the enormous task of providing funds for the group. Some person with a business connection or who is capable of making one should be chosen for this position. He must establish the credit of the group with the business men of the city and even with the audience.

The latter feel that if they pay in their annual admission fee, they must get something in return. Choose a man who can "put it over."

The failure of so many little theatres in this country has been due to two main causes: choice of plays and lack of a business head.

The first cause can be overcome by appointing a play-choosing committee which understands the taste of the supporting audience. How absurd is the idea of presenting Euripides, Ibsen, Shaw, Wilde, Dunsany, Maeterlinck, not to mention Schnitzler, Musset, Hervieu, Chekhov, etc. when the audience demands "The Little Minister," "Bought and Paid For," "Uncle Tom's Cabin," or a "Kentucky Colonel." Certainly the latter would not be given, but a compromise can be reached over which even artists will not have to blush.

The second cause is to be overcome by choosing a business manager for the theatre who can be relied upon and by permitting him to place the organization upon a business basis.

The first necessity of business system is to make out a budget for the season. Two hundred and fifty members at $20 each will net the group $5,000 for the season with a possible $1,000 more from the sale of seats. Deducting rent, light, heat, insurance, printing and other overhead expenses, the group will be allowed some $450 to $500 for each performance.

At the end of the season a complete audit must be made of all books and an itemized statement of the financial condition of the organization must be made to the members.

There is no reason why the Community Playhouse cannot be placed on as firm a business basis as any commercial theatre provided the right methods are used and the right people are at the head of it. Indeed it can be made more stable, inasmuch as it is sure of an audience and an income before it begins its season. This the commercial theatre lacks.

Not the least important functionaries are the *Committees*. Their appointment should be made with care and discretion. Appointments of committees are usually made by the president after consultation with the director. Here the result of careful choosing of the players' group will become manifest, for there must be in your group enough people of varying talent to committee a play from its reading to its first performance.

No director has time to read the enormous number of plays necessary to make choice for production. He cannot burden his mind or use his time in this way. There must be a sifting process, and this is provided for by a *Play Reading Committee*. Original plays are read by them and, if worthy of production are brought to the attention of the *Play Choosing Committee* at the head of which is the director.

The play reading committee will also present to the play choosing committee, at certain intervals, a list of the best plays it has read during the period, and the play choosing committee will in turn pick the best of this list. Thus the work of the director is greatly lessened.

There will be a *Publicity Committee* working with the business manager; also a *Finance Committee*. There should also be a *Dance Committee* to assist the director in plays requiring interpretive dancing; and the very important committees of *Staging* and *Lighting*.

In like manner there must be a *Costume Committee* headed by the art-director, who will design all costumes, and work out details of historical periods. The committee will either make the costumes or turn them over to assistants. The approval of the director will of course be secured on all designs before the costumes are actually made.

After the performance, costumes must not be thrown away; but must be turned over to the *Wardrobe Committee* who will store them in the theatre's wardrobe in numbered boxes.

Other committees of value that may be appointed are: Committees on *Voice*, *Diction*, *Miniature Stage Sets*, *Posters and Designs*, *Membership*, *Files*, *Lectures*, *Bookshelf*, *Musicales* and *Entertainment*.

The organization itself and the size of the city in which it is formed will determine the number of committees appointed. It is well to remember, however, that a committee with a definite thing to do usually does it, while matters that are left to an overworked individual may or may not be done. The more members of the group that can be kept busy, the more interest will be taken.

The following arrangement will give an adequate idea of the organization:

## ORGANIZATION

*Executive*
Business Manager
President
Vice-President
Secretary
Treasurer

*Production*
Director
Art Director
Stage Manager
Dance Director

## COMMITTEES

Membership
Play-Reading
Play-Choosing
Publicity
Finance
Wardrobe
Poster-Designer
Files
Lectures
Bookshelves

Musicales
Entertainment
Dance
Staging
Lighting
Costume
Music
Voice
Direction

## BIBLIOGRAPHY ON ORGANIZATION AND THEORY

BEEGLE, MARY P. and CRAWFORD, J. R. *Community Drama and Pageantry*. Yale University Press, 1916.

BURLEIGH, LOUISE. *The Community Theatre*. Little, Brown, Boston, 1917.

CHENEY, SHELDON. *The Art Theatre*. Knopf, N. Y., 1917.

CLARK, BARRETT H. *How to Produce Amateur Plays*. Little, Brown, Boston, 1917.

DICKINSON, THOMAS H. *The Insurgent Theatre*. Huebsch, N. Y., 1917.

MACGOWAN, KENNETH and ROBERT EDMOND JONES. *Continental Stagecraft*. Harcourt, Brace & Co., N. Y., 1922.

MACKAY, CONSTANCE D'ARCY. *The Little Theatre in the United States*. Holt, N. Y., 1917.

MODERWELL, HIRAM KELLY. *The Theatre of To-day*. John Lane, N. Y., 1919.

## IV

## THE AUDIENCE

THE theatre of to-day is fundamentally the same as the theatre of former times. Ancient Greece went to the theatre for diversion; Rome declared a holiday in order to turn loose her emotions; Mediæval Europe staged her pageants for the love of frolic: one and all went to see life as it ought to be and not as it really is—that is, the great mass of people did. The absurdities of Shakespeare's kings are apparent off the stage, but who does not find them convincing as played even by second-rate artists on the other side of the footlights? There were thinkers and scientists and artists in those times just as there are to-day, but the thinker, the scientist and the artist, as long as his taste is not too badly offended, loses, to a certain degree, his individuality in the theatre audience. There his emotions predominate. He loses, in a way, his sophistication, his critical powers, and becomes as a wondering child. But even a child has his likes and dislikes.

In his "Insurgent Theatre," Mr. Thomas H. Dickinson says of the modern audience: "The audience upon which any man of the theatre must depend for support of his productions is incoherent, inconsistent, and not as yet awakened to its powers and responsibilities. Studying the potential audience of the American theatre, we find that it falls roughly into the following classes:

"Puritans: To these the theatre is still forbidden. Though they attend it, they look upon it with suspicion. Even when they go they hold themselves rigidly and take no real pleasure in it. This is a very large group and of all the most influential.

"Theatre-Goers: To these the theatre is a pastime only, and all theatres are in one class whether legitimate, motion-picture or vaudeville theatre. Either their tastes have not been developed or, as is more likely, they check their taste at the cloakroom when they go to the theatre. This also is a large class.

"Connoisseurs: By some these are called 'high-brows.' They have become so critical and expert in their attitude toward a play as to be of little service in its support. This is a small but troublesome group.

"Theatre-Lovers: These are to be distinguished from the theatre-goers because they have taste, and from the connoisseurs because they go to the theatre to enjoy it and not to judge it. This class, which is very small, is largely made up of foreigners, Germans, French and Italians."

While this classification is very rough, it serves in a way to designate the types that attend the average commercial theatre. Which one of these types will the Community Playhouse attempt to draw around it?

Clearly it cannot hope to subsist on the theatre-lovers, for they are usually poor in purse and few in number. The group will of necessity have to look to the other classes.

The idea that a group can form and produce plays without any consideration of an audience is absurd. The Washington Square Players boasted of having done this. They wished to express themselves in their own way, and they put this desire into effect. But the Washington Square Players had the whole of New York City to draw from, and surely among six millions of people there ought to be enough of similar taste to form a small audience.

This is not to depreciate the work of the Washington Square Players; it is meant merely to emphasize the fact that every group can find a public. Not *the* public, to be sure. There is no such thing as *the* public. There is a collection of publics— *the publics*, but that high and mighty term, The Public, which has terrified artists for ages, is simply a misnomer. In the field of dramatics, there is a vaudeville public, a motion-picture public, a musical comedy public, a burlesque public and, with distinctions, a drama public. The question that faces the artist is: Can the tastes of these various publics be changed and improved?

Mr. Sam Losh of Fort Worth, Texas, prominent in the Southwest as a community song-leader, is of the opinion that the tastes of the people do not change. "I do not attempt any more to give the masses grand opera," he told me once, "for the simple reason that it disgusts them. However, I do not give them cheap popular songs. I get them to singing the best popular songs, something without offense in the words, and with a good swinging melody. I have worked with groups for years and those groups that started out favoring a certain type of song stuck to that type. At the end of four or five years they were singing it much better than when they began, but it was the same type. You cannot lead them away."

There is much truth in this statement. If your group is located in a large city where you can pick a public of any degree, well and good. If it is in a small place where your choice is limited, your theatre will fail, as many another such venture has, if you attempt to force down the throats of the commercial, the illiterate, and the indifferent, the diet of perception and thought.

Your audience then demands first consideration. Who are the people to support you? Have you an educated, art-appreciative group of five hundred or more who will back the best in drama, or will your audience be composed of the coarser-grained with limited appreciative capacity?

The kind of audience will determine the kind of plays, but first it will determine the kind of organization you are to have.

Suppose, as a promoter, you approach a commercial man and say to him: "I want you to take out a membership in our Community Playhouse. We are going to produce only the highest type of plays. We intend to incorporate the ideas of the foremost colorists and designers. The new type of staging will be used exclusively. We want you to take out a membership in our group." For your trouble he will probably laugh at you.

If, on the other hand, you emphasize the community spirit of the theatre, compare it to a municipal band or a park, show how it will be a factor in the settlement of the industrial unrest, and then suggest to him that he might buy one ticket—a single ticket for each performance of the season, the probability is that you will add a guarantor to your list.

This is merely a suggestion.    Individual groups must work out their own system of getting guarantors.    There are several methods used by Little Theatres to recruit audiences and hold them together, the two chief ways being by ticket guaranteeing and by taking the audience into the players' group as supporting members.    The latter method, while it gives a larger group to draw upon for committees, loses its effectiveness by making the group unwieldy.    It is probably a little more democratic, but at the same time it involves all the complications of democracy, with its politics and jealousies, offering little in return.    The former method seems to work better.

The Wisconsin Players accept the audience into membership, giving them the names of Supporting Members, Contributing Members, Regular Members, and Junior Members, with annual fees of $25, $10, $5 and $2 respectively.    One membership includes husband and wife, but other members of the family must hold separate membership.

The Chicago Little Theatre had a supporting audience of some 400 members each of whom contributed $10 annually to the theatre and in return received a single admission to each regular performance of the theatre for the season.

The St. Louis Artists' Guild Little Theatre is supported by endowment and by subscription of public-spirited citizens. Its audience is limited to members of the Artists' Guild.

The Cleveland Playhouse is kept going by two types of membership—active and supporting. The active, of course, have some part in production. Fees are $10 for active and $25 for supporting members.

The Community Theatre of Hollywood, and the Community Players of Denver are likewise supported by the two types of members.

The Duluth Little Theatre has sixty supporting members who contribute $5 each annually to the theatre.

The Arts and Crafts Little Theatre of Detroit was also supported by subscription. Members of the audience were charged $12 a season, which gave them one admission to each regular performance. Teachers and student members were charged only $5 a season.

It is certain that a Community Playhouse cannot run without money; moreover, it must have a definite amount for the season in order to make out a budget. If it is not endowed, then the audience which it expects to secure will have to stand back of it. Individual groups will work out their individual needs, but the best plan seems to be that of a supporting audience of several hundred who will guarantee to buy a seat in the theatre for a season. This is not asking much of them. They would probably attend anyway, but it gives the players a security.

As a business principle, contracts should be made out between the players' group and each member of the audience. The usual, "I hereby agree to purchase—tickets, etc.," is a good form. Some members will pay in advance and others will pay at each performance. The business manager will work out his own plans.

Should the audience be represented in the players'

group? Decidedly. The supporters of the enter-
prise have a right to express their likes and dislikes.
Some Community Playhouses give their audiences
the privilege of submitting play lists and written
criticisms of the plays. In others, the supporting
members are represented by an advisory board,
elected by them, to confer with the executive board
of the players' group. Individual members of the
audience take up their questions with a member of this advisory board, which in turn takes up
the matter with the executive board of the group.
This is an excellent plan, since boards make good
buffers, and buffers tend to relieve the little jars
of an organization.

Perhaps it would be well, before closing this chapter on the Audience, to say a word on the question
of obtaining the backing of societies, leagues, fra-
ternities, etc.

Organized support of any kind, as long as it does
not obtrude itself upon the work of the players, is
always advantageous. The trouble, however, with
most women's clubs, mothers' leagues, art societies,
etc. is that they are interested in the project only so

long as it is beneficial to their organization. It should be made clear to them at the beginning that the playhouse is a distinct community project and that it is not created for the assistance of any other organization.

Finally, the promoter should clear his mind of any illusion that through his Community Playhouse he is going to reform completely the dramatic standards of his community, that he is going to be able to educate an audience sufficiently large to float the project to an appreciation of the work of the advanced Art Theatre ideals. I know of no city in the United States to-day which can hold the interest annually of enough support to keep an ultra-Art Theatre going, season in and season out. A scheme of this kind may be supported for a season or two; but the fate of the Chicago Little Theatre and the Detroit Arts and Crafts Theatre, the two most artistic ventures in this country hitherto, proves conclusively, to my mind at least, that the Art Theatre has as yet no place in this country. It may eventually have a place, but not until our money-seeking generations have been succeeded by a more leisurely, cultivated population. The most that any Community Playhouse can hope to do is to present the best of the type of plays its audience demands, occasionally throwing out a bait of something different and better, and trusting that at some future period its ideals will be effected.

## V

## THE BUILDING

No players' organization will become permanent unless it has a home. The old adage of the rolling stone applies as much to a company as to an individual. A group will accomplish little that is exceptional in the new stage-craft, which depends so much on equipment, unless it has a stage of its own. There is an influence about a playhouse that tends to develop professionalism or finished players, and no group wishes to plod along in the over-worked field of amateur dramatics.

The first difficulty in the way of securing a building is the expense of erecting or remodeling. Players are usually filled with more enthusiasm than their purses are with money. But if they have enthusiasm, coupled with an incentive for good hard work and undaunted courage, there is not the slightest reason why a building of some kind cannot be secured.

It is not necessary to choose a prominent location. It is better far to find an empty store-room or a deserted hall on some less pretentious street, and let your public come uninvited in. And they will come. If good work is being done, they will ferret out the location even if it is in the most wretched slum district in the city. Witness the location of the Neighborhood Playhouse in New York City in the settlement district on Henry Street. Its audience is recruited from every part of the city. They go, not because it is a social institution, but because the Neighborhood Playhouse gives these persons what they want. That, you may say, is what the commercial managers and the "movies" do, yet the public is dissatisfied with their achievements. The commercial managers and the "movies" do not, generally, give the people what they want. Rather these managers provide what they think the publics want (to most of them there is but one public) with the injunction: "Take it or leave it!"

The next question that arises in the mind of the promoter is the ownership of the building or lease. No one member of the group wants to feel personally responsible for the debts of the group or to be the victim of a lawsuit through a fire or property loss.

The organization as presented in this book offers the only sane solution of this problem. The players' group must form itself as a State corporation with laws, by-laws and directorate. In this way the entire group is responsible, all being stockholders and hence equally to be held to account. This is not a minor question as some groups seem to think, for a single fire or catastrophe involving the loss of several lives may otherwise cost a few zealous persons a fortune.

It is well before constructing a building or even leasing one to give this question due consideration.

The size and kind of building erected will, of course, depend on the money the group has to spend, or the luck they have in securing an old building. The oft-repeated example of the Prairie Playhouse of Galesburg, Illinois, which rose out of the ruins of a dilapidated saloon, the playhouse at Lake Forest, Illinois, made from a dwelling, the Little County Theatre, Fargo, N. D., product of an abandoned chapel, are reminders of what has been done. Enthusiasm and work can repeat the accomplishment. It is not necessary for you to start with a $90,000 structure. If money is available for a building of this kind, so much the better, but a store building remodeled, probably at a cost of not more than $2,000, will serve just as well. One of the most artistic little playhouses in this country, the Vagabond Theatre of Baltimore, is a remodeled store building.

The question naturally arises: What size shall we make our building? This, of course, depends entirely on the players, their possibilities, the size of the audience, whether the building is to be a new one or an old one remodeled, and even on State and city laws.

Can you afford to pay an excessive insurance rate for your theatre? Theatres seating more than 300 require special insurance. Again, theatres must be built under regulation in order to guarantee the safety of the audience. Law regulations in the smaller cities are not so stringent, but in New York, Chicago, Detroit, Cleveland and other large cities, they are well defined. Laws of regulation are of two classes: those that protect society socially and morally, and those that protect life and property. Not all plays written can be placed before the public, and in certain cities the police censorship has to be reckoned with. The protection of life and property is accomplished by regulating the width of aisles, the number of exits, the construction of the building, the fireproofing of scenery and curtains, etc. One reason why so many playhouses come into conflict with the law, is that the group rushes blindly into building without thought or preparation. Before you build, consult your city's building laws.

An investigation of the Community Playhouses of the country shows that the average seating capacity is 200. Many are much smaller, many are larger. Maurice Browne's Little Theatre at Chicago seated 91. The Vagabond Theatre of Baltimore seats 60; the Detroit Arts and Crafts Theatre,

250; the Little Theatre of Philadelphia, 420; and the Neighborhood Playhouse, 411.

The playhouse of the Wisconsin Players of Milwaukee is probably the largest of the kind in the country. It is a three-story building with an Old English tea room in the basement, run in connection with the theatre. The auditorium occupies the first floor, reading and club rooms for members of the organization are located on the second floor, and the ballroom for social entertainments and dance rehearsals takes up the third floor.

### THE AUDITORIUM

Whatever the decision may be in regard to the seating capacity, the building should be constructed or remodeled along artistic lines. Choose some one color to dominate. Make the auditorium expressive, distinct, and the front of the building as well. The architect, who has probably had more experience than you in decorating, should be encouraged to make suggestions. Utilize everybody. This will tend to arouse a general interest in the coming theatre.

Avoid, if possible, the use of a long store building; but, if nothing else is procurable, this will do. If the building is extremely long and the audience small, the stage can be built so as to leave a space behind it. This space can be partitioned off and made into costume, dressing, storage and other necessary rooms.

Make your theatre auditorium intimate. Balconies are not necessary and boxes, like kings for whom they were created, are going out of fashion. Decorations should be simple, tending to create an atmosphere. If possible the floor should be slanted or made into a series of raised platforms. The upholstery of the seats should be in keeping with the color scheme of the walls.

Oftentimes large old halls can be secured. At first sight, nothing might seem more useless, but in fact, nothing could be better. The Talma Club of Providence, of which Mr. Henry Barker is director, has solved this problem. The only building available for the club was an old armory 125 feet long and 75 feet wide with a stage at one end. A semi-circular wall was placed across the hall about 50 feet from the curtain line, making an intimate little auditorium seating 460. The remaining part of the hall was turned into an assembly room 60 x 75 feet, two small lobbies for entrance, and extra space for storage. These partitions are movable since the hall has to be used for other purposes, and can be taken down or put up at will. This, of course, necessitates quite a little work. A hall that could be used exclusively for theatre work, so that partitions could be made permanent, would be much better. But enterprising groups will overcome any difficulty.

The curtain covering the stage may be made of cloth, canvas or steel. In the larger cities fire regulations require fire-proof curtains. Whatever is used, the color must be in keeping with the interior. Cloth curtains, if made of good material and hung in folds, add richness to the auditorium. The lifting curtain adds a touch of professionalism, but if this is used advertisements must be strictly prohibited.

The proscenium arch, the frame around the curtain, may be square or oval according to the taste of the architect. It should measure at least 15 x 25 feet. The square proscenium seems to be in favor with playhouses.

Orchestra pit and footlights may or may not be installed. The tendency at present, in the smaller theatres, is to do away with both. However, effects can be got with footlights that cannot be obtained with the indirect method of stage illumination, and the orchestra, if rightly used, can play an important part in a production. Music between acts does away with the "restless" waits so prevalent in playhouse companies.

Little need be said about the entrance of the building. Several little theatres have a small reception-room but few have box-offices. Lobbies are not needed.

Behind the curtain the beginner is at a loss. What size shall the stage be? Where should one place the dressing-rooms, the "prop" rooms, the "Green" room, and the numerous other necessities of the modern playhouse stage? Where shall the laboratory workrooms be placed and what size shall they be? Much of this information depends on the size of the building and its shape.

In this chapter on the building for a players' group, and the following ones on the Stage and Scenery, I have outlined what the group ought to have rather than what it will probably be able to secure. Effective work can be done with very little equipment, and there is recompense in working against odds, but it stands to reason that a group of players, no matter what its ability, will give better performances if it has something with which to work. The votary of the Art Theatre who says that all commercial theatre-managers are loggerheads, and their methods bad, not only belittles himself, but proves that he is an amateur in the theatrical game. Most of the mechanical devices on the commercial stage to-day have been arrived at after many years of experimentation by practical men of the theatre. Some of them can be dispensed with by the playhouse worker; most of them, in simple form at least, are needed. The least a beginner can do is to know what they are and what their purpose is.

What little can be said about the construction of the stage will be taken up in the following chapter.

# VI

## THE STAGE

THE most important part of the Community Playhouse will now be considered—the stage. The suggestions that are made here are based upon a careful study of the stages of the most important playhouses in the country.

In the planning of a stage much depends on the
size of the building in which it is constructed, but
the chief point to be kept in mind by the prospective
builder is not to make his stage too small. Small-
ness makes for intimacy, it is true, but the disad-
vantages offset the gains. A number of playhouses
in the country are now working under the disadvantage of too small stages. Thirty feet long,
twenty feet wide, with six feet in the flies and, if
possible, sixteen feet, should be the minimum size
of the stage. It is almost impossible to create illusion on a smaller one; an attempt to group results in "bunching" and isolation is impossible.

Any group of players who have had the slightest
experience on the "platforms" which the average

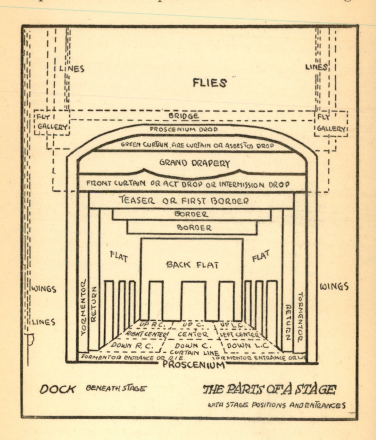

hall or college auditorium boasts of as a stage, knows the necessity of adequate room.

To the sides of the stage, in the wings, there must be at least four feet of free room on one side and ten feet on the other. Remembering that the prompter's desk, the instruments of thunder, lightning, etc., are usually just off stage, one at once sees the necessity of space.

The question of an "apron" or forestage is an individual one. Just now, among certain managers, there seems to be a rival of the old Shakespearean idea of the forestage. Livingston Platt and Granville Barker, representing the new staging methods, have recommended it. That it adds to the intimacy of the stage is undoubtedly true, but the necessarily restricted size of the auditorium of the Community Playhouse usually renders it impossible.

### STAGE CONSTRUCTION

For the actual building of the stage an architect and a carpenter will be consulted. However, it is just as well for the player to understand the construction and mystery of the platform on which he works.

There are several kinds of stages, drop, sliding, lifting, swing, revolving and stationary. The latter will probably be the kind used by a new group. The field of this book does not cover a discussion of these types of stages but confines itself to the stationary and portmanteau, the two used by all Little Theatres in this country.

The frame-work of the stage is constructed of re-enforced trestles, 3½ to 4 feet in height, placed about 2 feet apart. The floor, usually, is doubly laid, and oftentimes contains trap doors. The doubling of the floor enables it to bear heavy weights and keeps it from creaking, and trap-doors are used in such plays as "Hamlet" and "Faust." The whole of the frame-work is cross-tied and re-enforced.

## THE CYCLORAMA

A device introduced recently into the theatre is the cyclorama or horizont. Every Community Playhouse should have one of these devices. It is merely the rear wall of the stage made cylindrically concave and domed. Colored lights can then be played on this with startling effect. It is especially useful in producing sky effects and giving depth to the stage by illusion.

The following diagram shows its form:

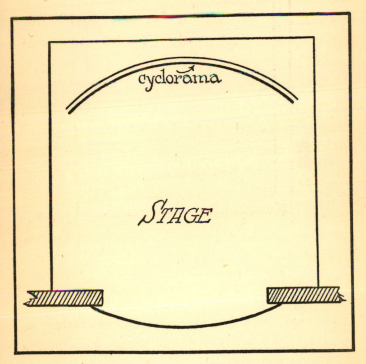

Diagram of cyclorama

I have planned for some time to make one of cloth and light enough to be easily portable. Its construction would be as follows:

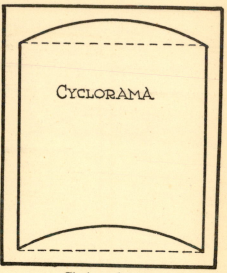

Cloth cyclorama

This has worked well on a miniature stage and should be useful if enlarged.

The cyclorama is still in its infancy. Its future is assured. Several of the Little Theatres in the country have already employed this device and the commercial theatres will follow shortly.

Whether the cyclorama is to remain of lath-and-plaster and is to be made stationary is a question. There are several drawbacks to this type, chief

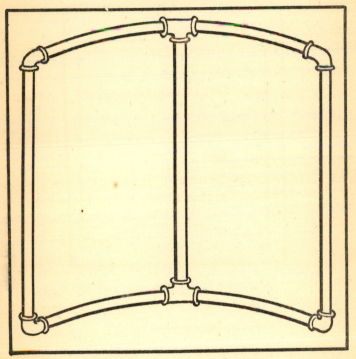

Gas pipes bent for cyclorama

among them being that the wall is in the way when scenery is to be moved on and off the stage and that the dome interferes with the gridiron and the flies. A German theatre has constructed a cyclorama which works on hinges and tilts back. A Swedish company has placed a cloth cyclorama on the market which rolls around a movable frame. This one is said not to tremble when in place, the chief objection to all other cloth cycloramas. Also, its surface is coated with a rough substance to refract the light rays much as the plaster model does.

If the players find it too expensive to construct a cyclorama of plaster, a substitute of cloth can be used, bending gas pipes as in the diagram shown on page 71 and covering them.

### DRESSING-ROOMS

Dressing-rooms, while not as important for the small theatre as for the commercial stage, must not be overlooked.

There should be at least four dressing-rooms in any playhouse and more in proportion to the size of the building. Occasionally they are placed behind the stage, sometimes to the right or left. More often they are above or below or in an adjoining

building. Wherever they are they must be connected by means of speaking tubes or electric flashes
with the prompter's desk. This is one item of
equipment which no small theatre should be without.

These rooms should be placed so that the sexes
need not thrust themselves on each other. This is
an act of courtesy, and modern theatres recognize
it. Each room should have good ventilation, and
sufficient light and heat. The rooms should be
tastefully decorated and kept attractive. In each
one there should be a wash-bowl, a stand with individual drawers, and as many mirrors as there are
persons to occupy the room. It is hardly possible
to provide a separate room in a Community Playhouse for each actor, but as many as possible should
be provided. If several persons are to use the same
room it is best to have a long table constructed,
seating, say, ten people, five on each side. Stools,
screwed to the floor may be placed on each side of
the table. In the centre, dividing the two sides,
there should be two rows of mirrors. Above each
mirror there should be a small electric light, and be-

low it, buried in the table, another one.   This arrangement will give a lighting similar to that of the stage, provided that direct illumination is used on the latter.   The player can tone his make-up in accordance.

### THE GREEN ROOM

No Community Playhouse should be without its Green Room.   This is the room where all the players can meet and be provided with coffee, cigarettes and periodicals.   This room also should be connected with the prompter's desk by a speaking-tube.   It will, of course, be provided with chairs, tables, etc., and, most certainly a full-length mirror in order that players may have a final survey of their costumes before making a stage entrance.

### VENTILATION

There must be at least one ventilator in the roof just above the flies.   This will not only keep the atmosphere behind the curtain pure, but it will often aid in stopping back-stage fires.   This ventilator should be made to open and close and should be manipulated by a rope or mechanical worm. It should be constructed so as not to permit drafts, but at the same time to provide plenty of fresh air. This can be accomplished by placing a hood over the mouth.

## MOVABLE STAGES

Nothing has been said thus far about a form of stage that is being used by several players' groups in this country. I refer to the portmanteau stage as inaugurated by Mr. Stuart Walker of New York and developed by other workers.

Here the enterprising Mr. Barker of the Talma Players again takes the lead in inventiveness, for he has in his workshop two portmanteau theatres of his own design. One of them is invariable as to size.

The stage consists of twelve parallels, each two feet high with a 3 x 9 foot surface. These are clamped together with an enclosing parallel, 12 x 27 feet, and set up on castors so that the entire stage can be rolled about at will. A proscenium arch, 13 x 22 feet, is attached, as are also back and side

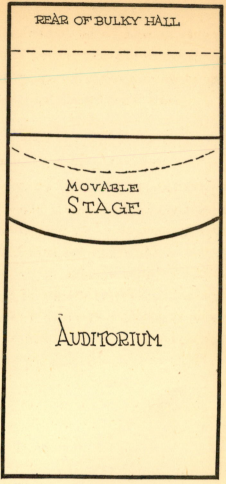

Diagram showing how a movable
stage was placed in a bulky hall

skeleton-frames to hold border lights and borders. A stage front, which can be regulated in size to fit the building in which it is placed, is made in several sections. There are extra parallels to increase, if necessary, the size of the stage. A stage of this sort can, of course, be set up in any room sufficiently large where, as is frequently the case, conditions do not permit of nails or attachments of any kind to the room itself.

The other portmanteau stage is similar, with the exception that it can be varied as to height and depth, and the enclosed off-stage space may be extended indefinitely. Both these stages are lighted by a movable switchboard mounted on castors, and changed from place to place as desired.

# VII

## SCENERY

THE worker in the theatre is probably familiar with the kinds of scenery used; this chapter is primarily for the beginner.

Just above a plane parallel with the floor of the stage and up even with the top of the proscenium arch is the region of the stage known as the *Flies*. Here certain kinds of scenery are kept in position, to be lowered or raised as needed. These are known to stage hands as the roller-drops, flat-drops and borders.

*Roller-Drops* appear to the audience as curtains. They are really large painted pieces of canvas which are wound up and down on rollers whose ends are fastened in the *Gridiron*, a large steel framework in the flies, and operated by means of ropes run through pulleys above the rollers and then down to the stage floor.

*Flat-Drops* are made of canvas on huge wooden

frames, usually a little higher than the proscenium opening. They are raised and lowered into place in the better equipped theatres by means of electrical apparatus, smaller theatres operating them by hand with ropes. When drops of this kind are used it is necessary to make the region in the flies where they are kept even greater than the height of the stage, since the frame must be lifted out of sight.

The *Borders* are usually constructed in a similar manner, but are much shorter in length. They are used to produce sky effects, to serve as ceilings, foliage, etc.

These three types constitute overhead or disappearing scenery. They are reached in the "loft" by means of ladders which run up from the stage floor to the gridiron.

### INTERIORS

More familiar to the theatre-goer is the interior "flat." This is the type of scenery used to make walls forming rooms. Flats are made of light wooden frames covered with canvas. They are of various sizes according to the size of the stage and the place where the piece is used. To form a room these flats are placed with their edges together, lashed and braced on the back side. Flats are used also in exteriors such as for building houses, store fronts, etc.

Just inside the proscenium arch stand two strips of scenery, one on each side of the stage, and usually with a third piece, a border, stretched across the top. The two strips are called *Tormentors* and the particular border the *Teaser*. These pieces are movable and are used to enlarge or diminish the opening of the stage. The tormentors are usually made of thin solid wood and covered with canvas.

### EXTERIORS

Flat pieces for exterior scenes are generally made similar to pieces for interior sets. Tree trunks, well curbings and pieces of that nature, are either made hollow of light lath or of wire net and covered with canvas. Stage rocks are made by folding daubed canvas over boxes.

Floating scenery in exteriors such as branches and foliage are held in position by a coarse gauze. These gauzes are often used to produce mist effects.

The beautiful forest scene of "Chanticler" was created through a skillful use of gauzes.

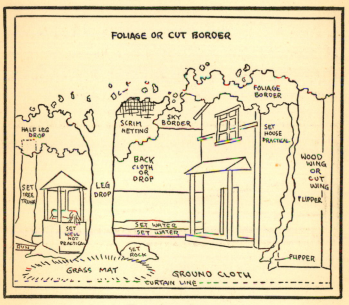

Exterior pieces

### MATS

Floor mats are used both in interior and exterior scenes. In interiors a large rug is often used; for exteriors a green cloth or grass mat may represent the earth. Care must be taken in placing these,

for the slightest wrinkle may cause a player to turn
his tragedy into a farce.

### RUNS

Runs are inclined planes, usually placed outside
of doors so that when the actor moves away his
ascent or descent gives the appearance of adding
distance between himself and the audience.

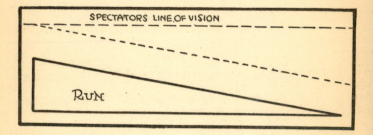

### CURTAINS

Community Playhouses may use either a canvas
curtain or a draped one.  The expensive steel curtain of the commercial theatre is unnecessary.

If it is made of canvas, the curtain is operated in
the manner of a drop.  If of drapery, it may part
in the centre sliding half each way, folded by ropes
or lifted.  It must be kept in mind that curtains are

regulated by city law, and before deciding definitely on any one kind you should become acquainted with the regulations of your city.

Experiments in adjustable prosceniums and novelty curtains are being made every year, but the beginner should keep to the trodden paths until he has learned the art of the stage. Much can be acquired from books but the great lessons are to be found in experimentation.

### BIBLIOGRAPHY ON SCENERY AND STAGE SETTING

*Art of Scene Painting.* By practical scenic artists. French, N. Y., 1879.

ATKINSON, FRANK H. *Scene Painting and Bulletin Art.* Drake, Chicago, 1916.

BAKSHY, ALEKSANDR. *Path of the New Russian Stage.* Luce, Boston, 1918.

BROWNE, VAN DYKE. *Secrets of Scene Painting and Stage Effects.* Dutton, N. Y., 1913.

CHENEY, SHELDON. *The Art Theatre.* Knopf, N. Y., 1917.

CHESSHIRE, JOHN K. C. *Bethlehem Tableaux from Behind the Scenes.* Dent, London, 1913.

CLARK, BARRETT H. *How to Produce Amateur Plays.* Little, Brown, Boston, 1917.

CRAIG, GORDON. *Toward a New Theatre*. Dutton, 1913.

FLICKINGER, ROY C. *The Greek Theatre and its Drama*. University of Chicago Press, 1918.

HAMILTON, CLAYTON. *Studies in Stagecraft*. Holt, N. Y., 1914.

LLOYDS, F. *Practical Guide to Scene Painting*. Rowney, London, 1879.

KROWS, ARTHUR EDWIN. *Play Production in America*. Holt, N. Y., 1916.

MACGOWAN, KENNETH. *The Theatre of To-morrow*. Boni & Liveright, N. Y., 1921.

MACKAY, CONSTANCE D'ARCY. *Costume and Scenery for Amateurs*. Holt, N. Y., 1915.

MATTHEWS, BRANDER. *A Book About the Theatre*. Scribner, N. Y., 1916.

MODERWELL, HIRAM KELLY. *The Theatre of To-day*. Lane, N. Y., 1914.

PALMER, JOHN LESLIE. *The Future of the Theatre*. Bell, London, 1913.

PRICE, WILLIAM THOMPSON. *The Technique of the Drama*. Brentano, N. Y., 1909.

RENTON, EDWARD. *The Vaudeville Theatre: Building, Operation and Management*. Gotham Press (Inc.), N. Y., 1918.

SACHS, EDWARD O. *Stage Construction*. Batsford, London, 1898.

STRATTON, CLARENCE. *Producing in Little Theatres*. Holt, N. Y., 1921.

*Theatrical Scene Painting*. Appleton Pub. Co., Omaha, Neb., 1916.

# VIII

## MAKING OF SCENERY

For every play there must be special scenery.  Let the beginner get that fixed in his mind.  Only amateurs and cheap stock companies use the same settings over and over again without change.  It is not absolutely necessary that pieces should be made new, but they must be so arranged and added to that they will not be recognized as the setting of a former play.

The first requirement for the making of scenery is a miniature stage—an exact copy of the larger stage, and made in proportion.  It may be 10 x 20 inches in size; it may be 3 x 5 feet, but it should be at least large enough to get results.

The theatre artist designs the scene on paper and gives his sketch to the director or scenery committee.  It is then passed on, and, if approved, made into scenery for the miniature stage.

Scenery for the miniature stage is usually made of cardboard, clay or wood pieces painted with water colors. The artist experiments with lights and colors until the desired effects are produced.

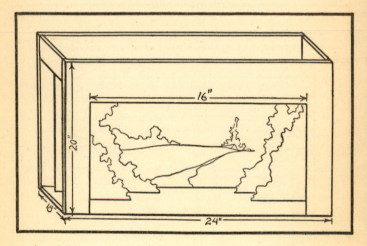

A miniature stage to be used by the playhouse worker for experimentation.

The miniature set approved, he enlarges his scale of figures to full stage-size and turns the plans over to the stage carpenter.

Thus there is no guessing at results.

## FLATS

The frames of flats are made of white pine strips, 2½ to 4 inches in width by 1 inch in thickness, according to the size of the piece. Height will range

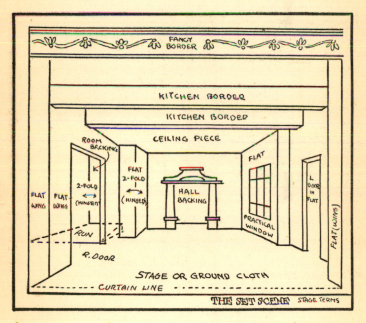

from 14 to 30 feet according to the height of the proscenium arch.

The frame of the flat is made similar to that of a cheap screen door, the ends of the strips being mor-

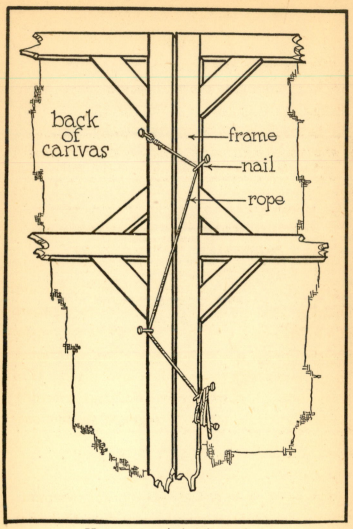

back
of
canvas

frame

nail

rope

How scenery is laced together

tised and nailed.    Cross strips are also mortised and nailed.    Corners are bracketed.

Ordinary flax canvas is used to cover the frames, being drawn tightly over them and tacked on the rear side.    Flats go in sets and in preparation for storage in the *Dock* (the storage room beneath the stage), are numbered according to the piece, and labeled with the act, scene and play in which they were last used.

## BACK DROPS

For the back drops and borders which use wide areas of cloth, seams are necessary.    Such seams are made by glueing the edges of the strips together. If a roller drop is used the upper edge of the canvas is tacked to the roller, and a heavy batten fastened on the lower edge to keep the canvas tight.    If a frame drop is used, a huge frame of the size needed is constructed, similar to the frame of the flat, and the canvas is tacked taut.

## PRIMING

The canvas at this point is ready for treatment. The first step is priming.    A quantity of whitening

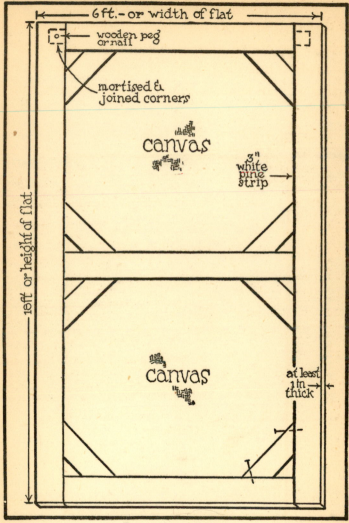

Rear view of flat

Labels within figure:
- 6 ft.– or width of flat
- wooden peg or nail
- mortised & joined corners
- canvas
- 3" white pine strip
- 18 ft. or height of flat
- canvas
- at least 1 in thick

is dissolved in water and sizing is added. As few sizings are of the same strength, experiment must be made before the priming is applied. Too little sizing will not hold the whitening and the scene will rub off.

Priming will leave the surface white.

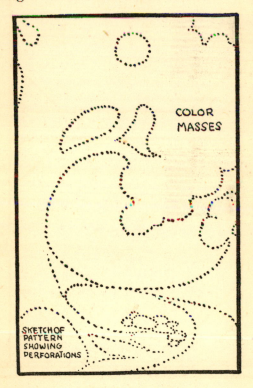

### PATTERNS

In the meantime the artist or his assistants have enlarged patterns on manila paper from the miniature set. The lines and masses of color are outlined with perforations about an inch apart. These patterns are then laid on the white scenery and dusted with a bag of fine charcoal which leaves the necessary outlines. Artists of experience often dispense with the patterns and sketch free hand.

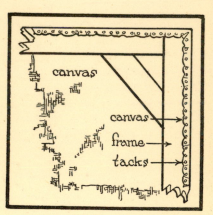

Method used in tacking canvas

Colors are next applied. The first coat is merely a filling in of the large masses with their predominating color.    Details are eliminated, and only broad effects are aimed at.    The colors, which are prepared by adding water, are first tried out on white canvas to test the shade before they are applied to the scenery.

Since pigment colors do not appear the same by artificial light as by sunlight the artist in the Community Playhouse will have to experiment considerably on his miniature stage before attempting to color his scenery on the larger one.

## IX

## DESIGNING SCENERY

THERE are three kind of scenery, broadly speaking, used on the stage to-day—realistic, impressionistic and conventional.　All three types are used both on the commercial and playhouse stages.　The tendency, however, with such forces to support them as Robert Edmond Jones and Joseph Urban, is toward the latter two.

### REALISTIC SCENERY

Realistic scenery is just what its name implies. Following the old wing idea of stage setting, producers in Europe and in this country became possessed with the idea of making the stage appear just as close to nature as possible.　Interior sets were made, to the finest detail, like the room they were to represent; exteriors were supposedly a photograph of nature.　But nature cannot be copied with wire netting and plaster, and shaking walls give the lie to realistic interiors.

Certain it is that realistic scenery is not real to the audience, nor does it produce the effect of reality. But in the hands of a Belasco or an Ames it can be used very effectively.

Perhaps the players' group will be compelled to use old stage sets at the beginning, or will have to make sets that require realistic handling.

The requisites for scenery of this kind are simplicity and true illusion. In the remodeling of your interiors or the making of them, bear in mind that illusion must be complete. Door frames should never be represented by painting. They must be built in of real wood. Likewise the door itself will be a real door with real hinges, a real knob and a real lock. Window sashes, while the glass may be simulated by using a fine bright gauze, should be of wood, and should be weighted if they are to be opened. The window frame will be built in. Walls must be braced and steadied so that the slamming of doors or a gust of wind will not cause them to quiver.

Borders used as ceilings must be dispensed with if possible and regular ceilings stretched.   Chandeliers will be braced to keep them from swinging to and fro when the heavy man crosses the stage.   All fantastic decorations of the side walls will be left out. Unless the scene actually demands something different, it is far better to have walls in a solid color harmonizing with the mood of the particular scene. A fine stenciled border merely to set off, is sufficient.

Pictures should not be hung about; they make the room look patchy.

The furniture, needless to say, must be real, and heavy or light in construction according to the type of the room.   If your play is a period play do not use furniture belonging to some other period.   Color of wood and upholstering on the set must harmonize with the wall coloring.   Tables should be 30 inches high, and chairs, unless for some particular effect, 18 inches.   Floor covering for interiors will be dark. All windows and doors which face the audience will be backed with scenery.

Keep this suggestion in mind; the adding of details will not make your scene more realistic, but will confuse the mind of the audience. It is the general impression that counts. A "solid" interior is effected by making the chief articles in the room bulky; "light" room by providing it with light, slender furniture, delicate door and window casings and plenty of windows.

In designing interiors it is well to study actual rooms of character. Certain rooms seem to speak. Study recesses, bay-windows, stairs, French-windows, fireplaces.

Players with slender means can use scenery over and over again by making slight alterations. A fresh coat of paint, a window moved, a door in a new position, will turn the set into an entirely different room.

In realistic exterior scenes, do not try to copy nature. Plan broad effects and make lights do the rest.

And now there is one subject in connection with the designing of scenery that must be emphasized—perspective. This has caused designers and theatre men more trouble than any other factor.

The theatre stage offers at most 30 feet of space

and it is necessary in many scenes to give the effect of huge distances. This would be simple enough if the actor did not have to move back and forth on the stage. The scene designer can so construct his lines by means of mechanical illusion and by lights as to suggest distances. But the actor fails to diminish in size as he moves from the audience and with the suggested perspective of distance of the scenery before the eyes of the audience he begins to grow in stature until by the time he has reached the rear of the stage he looks like a giant. Of course the skillful use of receding runs aids somewhat, but the illusion is never complete. This is one technical problem that the stage has never been able to solve, and one that is likely to baffle producers always.

The invention of the cyclorama or horizont has done much to assist the designer. The concave dome shape of this background and ceiling, producing no lines, does much, when it is played on by lights, to trick the eyes of the audience. This property is of especial value in the suggestion of sky and cloud effects. Moving picture clouds can be played upon this white lineless background, assisted by flood lights, spots and tapers, giving the semblance of the great outdoors with limitless expansion. Inasmuch as there are no lines, there is no perspective and the diffusive light, baffling to the gaze of the spectator, forms a quivering mass of suggestion.

## IMPRESSIONISTIC SCENERY

A new stagecraft has come into the theatre. It is known as the "new art," the "decorative movement," "impressionism," etc. In truth it is only the presence of the creative artist. Reality is sought, but it is the reality produced by mood and suggestion—and these are produced by simple beauty and by emphasis on the important and the motif of the scene.

It is not my purpose in this book to enter deeply into a discussion of the principles of the new stagecraft. The fact is, the principles are not well understood, even by those artists who are experimenting, and many of the latter refute the statements of others. Certain tendencies, however, are evident.

Simplicity of design is the basis. There is no attempt to give a photographic record in any sense.

Decorative line and mass are used to the exclusion of the ornate. Perspective is obtained not by painted line but by plastic objects thrown in light and shadow by means of lighting and color. The scene is suggested, not photographically reproduced, for suggestion and not representation is at the bottom of art.

There is none of the glaring artificiality about impressionistic settings that is so prevalent in the realistic. It is as if one viewed a scene by the low moon. Masses of black tree trunks, outlined against the yellow horizon, and towering lines of an old church steeple mounting heavenwards. Beauty enough and to spare! It differs from nature in that a particular object, the most important part of the scene, is emphasized. It clearly stands out and dominates the setting.

An impressionistic setting is not chosen hit or miss. It is designed for a particular scene of the play, and it is designed for a purpose—to heighten the particular emotion or motif of that scene. Thus an impressionistic setting of Maeterlinck's tombs

would strive to give the effect of emptiness, hollow-
ness, loneliness.

## ITS DIVISIONS

The new stagecraft has divided itself into two
lines, that which has just been mentioned—the development of suggestion with its decorative appeal
and motif; and the subordination of scenery of any
kind to acting. This latter variety is of an even
more plastic type. Perspective of any kind is done
away with; backgrounds are kept negative and neutral and the actor is brought into prominence. The
leading exponent of this type is Gordon Craig.
Those who favor this line of work in its different
branches deal exclusively with flat-colored screens
or curtained backgrounds. The stage may be hung
completely round with curtains, neutral in color, and
is then supposed to represent any scene that the play
demands. The actor is the chief element; he pre-
dominates, and the curtains are for the purpose of
throwing him into even greater prominence.

Screens are constructed much like flats, but are

covered with heavier material, and usually several are hinged together.

This method of staging is, however, passing. The more advanced playhouses have gone beyond it. It still finds favor in college dramatic clubs and among amateur companies.

## CONVENTIONAL SCENERY

Conventional designs do not mean old-fashioned groove-worn sets.  They are merely simple, artistic designs expressing a purpose.  Like the impressionistic settings they depend on suggestion, but it is suggestion by definite line and form.  A striking boldness of detail is to be seen.  Conventional scenery is to the impressionistic what the cartoon is to the painted picture.  There is something exaggerated, disproportionate and sketchy about it.  The attempt is made, not to reproduce, but rather to represent by hinting the central idea.  Subtlety of color and motif are ignored.  Broad effects are aimed at, both in form and color, with an obvious suggestion of the mood of the particular scene or play.   Lee Simonson, who did a great deal of designing for the Washington Square Players, is one of the leading advocates in America of this type of setting.

# X

## LIGHTING

More and more on the modern stage the effectiveness of lighting has come to the front. By means of spot-lights, footlights, little jets and tapers, a whole desert is made to appear in a few feet's space.

There are two methods of stage lighting—direct and indirect. Up to the time when the lighting artist came into the theatre practically all the lighting was direct. Footlights, floods, spots and borders served. Only within recent years has the subject of lighting been given serious thought. Only within very recent years has it become an art.

The old system of illumination seemed to be: lights in full blast for comedy, and dimmed for tragedy; and for anything else in proportion. Modern stagecraft makes lighting an art, subtle, diffusive and penetrating. The artist's brush is surpassed, for lights can paint stage pictures far more beautiful and with more emotional effect on the audience; the actor's art is rivaled, for the subtlety of color, light and shade, affect the senses of the spectator as much as the human voice; and the soul of the dramatist's play can be mirrored by the playing of a single light across the stage.

The tendency is to do away with footlights, since they produce an unnatural illumination. Borders, which were created to kill the shadows made by the foots are now attacked by artists who maintain that the absence of shadows on the stage greatly destroys illusion. In real life light comes from one certain point. Consequently there are always lights and shades, and these lights and shades are what make human beings appear solid. Whatever the arguments may be for and against, certain it is that the new methods of lighting have produced a marked effect on the stage, both in the playhouses and in the commercial theatres.

In building or remodeling your theatre, unless you have had experience with the indirect lighting system, it is best to install the direct also.

There should be at least three rows of lights

in the *footlights*, set, preferably, in a semi-circular shallow trough, backed by white painted tin. This trough should be placed near the edge of the forestage, and the tin run high enough to keep the light from shining in the auditorium. One of these rows should be of blue, one of amber, and the other of green. Bulbs should be placed about 8 inches apart. Each row should have its own dimmer, a device for regulating the intensity of light.

*Border-lights*, which are attached in the flies, should be placed between each drop, with one just behind the proscenium arch. These will likewise contain blue, amber and green bulbs. Border light bulbs are usually placed 6 to 8 inches apart on strips half the length of the stage, and can be lowered or raised by means of ropes. They should be backed by bright reflectors, and each border provided with a dimmer.

*Strip-lights* are similar to border lights in construction with the exception that they can be moved about to any part of the stage and connection made to plugs. *Bunch-lights* serve the same purpose and are operated much in the same way.

At least one *flood light* should be in the equipment. There should be a number of these. They are, of course, movable and can be placed on any part of the stage, behind drops, up in the flies, or wherever is most effective. *A spot-light* is usually worked from the rear of the house, but may be manipulated from the stage anywhere from the floor to the loft. Spot and flood lights are usually high candle-power lights with powerful reflectors behind them and an apparatus attached to focus the light. Stereopticans are sometimes used to serve this purpose.

The primary colors of lighting are red, blue and green. By combining any of these colors in given proportions, any color of light may be produced. Thus yellow may be produced from red and green, purple from red and blue, and so on. This applies only to lights, not to pigment colors.

Indirect lighting seems to be gaining favor with the artists of the stage. And so it should; for it removes at once one of the most disagreeable of all stage faults—glaring illumination. From the Italian architect, Fortuny of Venice, we got the

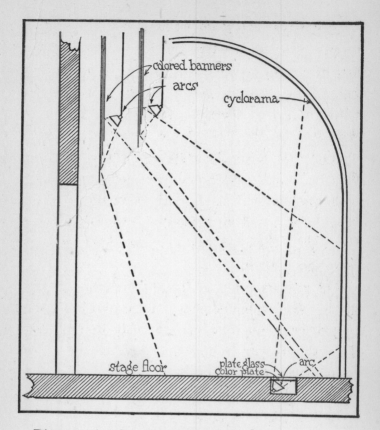

Diagram showing the working of the Fortuny system of indirect lighting. Light is thrown on colored banners from powerful arcs in the flies which in turn is reflected upon the stage in soft colors.

first contribution. Fortuny's method is simple. Very powerful arc-lights placed in the flies are directed on strips of black and white serried banners, which in turn reflect the light on the stage. Wonderful effects of "soft" lighting are thus obtained.

But there is a decided disadvantage in this method. Excessively high-powered arc-lights must be used in order to reflect sufficient light on the stage and the silk banners soon deteriorate by heat refraction. As a result the system becomes an expensive one both from the amount of electric current consumed and from the replacement of parts. Ingenious theatre men are getting by these obstacles by placing lower-powered lights behind filter screens of varying colors and throwing the light directly on the stage as in the accompanying illustration.

This, I believe, is the best system that can be adopted by workers in playhouses. It at once obviates the troublesome features of the Fortuny system, producing results almost equal in effect, and at the same time is within the limited means of most groups. If the playhouse will combine this latter system with spots, floods, high candle-power arcs in

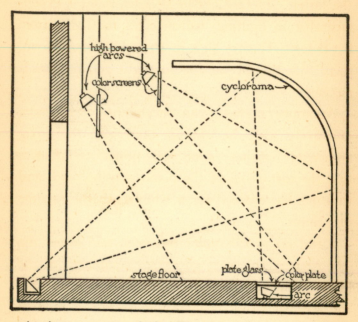

An improvement of the Fortuny system of lighting. The lights here are thrown through color screens, retaining the soft effect but eliminating the use of excessively powerful arcs and the use of banners.

the flies, backed by reflectors, the whole footlight and border system can be done away with.

The commercial theatre, recognizing the ineffectiveness of the footlight system, and the possibilities of the new methods of lighting, is swinging over to the latter.   In fact David Belasco, pioneer experimentalist in lighting, banished all footlights from his Belasco Theatre back in 1914.   It would seem, then, that the day of the footlight and borders is passing.

Atmospheric effects can be obtained much more effectively with the indirect than with the direct system of lighting.   One feels under its influence that the soft pedal of the piano is being used, and that one has escaped for a while from the ragtime jazz music.

Little up to this point has been said about the switchboard, the most important equipment of the lighting system.   It will probably not be possible for the beginning company to install a modern theatre board.   The one installed, however, must be ample; the entire lighting system of the theatre should go through it.   It should be placed on the prompter's side of the stage within speaking distance of the stage manager's desk, or connected with it by means of a speaking-tube.   A view of the stage is also necessary in order that the electrician can watch his effects. A large mirror can be placed just above the board at an angle, if it is necessary for the operator to have his back to the stage. The board itself on which the switches are placed, is usually of marble and can be constructed only by an expert electrician. The players must insist, however, that the entire electrical control equipment should be placed on it and that borders, footlights, strips, bunches and any other lights should have individual switches and dimmers if suitable effects are to be obtained.

By effect I do not mean the simple lowering of lights in a love scene, but a richer, fuller, artistic meaning.

Let me again impress on the beginner the importance of making a diligent study of lighting and its possibilities.

Says Mr. Moderwell in "The Theatre of To-day":

"Light seems a quivering, living thing to us. No other sensuous excitement, save possibly music, can seize and absorb our attention so completely. So, with certain sorts of drama, the newer producers have discovered how to make light represent the soul of the action itself, carrying us with it in its ebb and flow and giving us the sense of living in its inner life."

The lighting of a play is a psychological and temperamental matter as far as the audience is concerned. Its effects are as subtle as music, and can no more be explained. We only know that certain lights normally produce certain emotions under certain conditions. Why it has this hypnotic power and what that power is cannot be explained here.

Lighting in the theatre has become an art. The sooner the players' group realizes this, the better its productions will be.

### BIBLIOGRAPHY ON LIGHTING

BEEGLE, MARY PORTER and CRAWFORD, JACK RANDALL. *Community Drama and Pageantry*. Yale University Press, 1916.

BELL, LOUIS. *Art of Illumination*. McGraw, N. Y., 1902.

CLARK, BARRETT H. *How to Produce Amateur Plays*. Little, Brown, Boston, 1917.

KROWS, ARTHUR H. *Play Production in America*. Holt, N. Y., 1916.

LUCKIESH, M. *Lighting Art: Its Practice and Possibilities*. McGraw, N. Y., 1917.

MODERWELL, HIRAM KELLY. *The Theatre of To-day*. Lane, N. Y., 1914.

MOSES, MONTROSE J. *The American Dramatist*. Little, Brown, Boston, 1917.

NATIONAL X-RAY REFLECTOR CO. *Lighting from Concealed Sources*. National X-Ray Reflector Company, Chicago, 1919.

TAYLOR, EMERSON. *Practical Stage Directing for Amateurs*. Dutton, N. Y., 1916.

For list of magazine references on Lighting see:

GAMBLE, WILLIAM BURT. *The Development of Scenic Art and Stage Machinery*, a list of references in the New York Public Library. Public Library, N. Y., 1920.

# XI

## PRODUCTION

FOR production there must be a producer. In play work this means the director and his assistant, the stage-manager. Upon these two rests the burden of the preparation of the finished product.

The director of the Community Playhouse need not be a professional actor. In fact, some of the best producing work in the country has been done by directors of little or no professional experience. The average professional director tends to make puppets out of his players and the spontaneous spirit of amateur acting is lost. At best, the professional director can only give his cast a gloss of professionalism, and the coloring is bound to show through in spots.

But whether a professional or an amateur, the director must be a tactful individual with a fund of ideas and a fine instinct for production. He must know how to gain scene and individual "emphasis"; he must understand "stage movement," "values," "pauses," "rhythm," and "tempo." He must know these tools and, further, how to use them. He must have a knowledge of mechanics and its possibilities, and certainly he must have a working knowledge of "grouping" and "color." He must not only know these things; he must know them so much better than his players that there will never be any discussion about his decisions.

The stage-manager, his assistant, has been termed a "director in the making." The phrase is apt, for this is just what he is.

As soon as the play is decided upon for the group, the director and the stage-manager get together and make a careful study of it. Each character is studied closely, even if he has but a dozen words to speak. The type of man and his characteristics, according to the play, are noted, and a member of the group is chosen for the part.

The director must know what each one of his players can do. In order to get this information, private try-outs should be held, giving each member

a range of parts.    Every player works best in parts
of a certain type.    Some young girls, because they
make a pretty picture on the stage, fit excellently
into parts that require nothing more than this.
Likewise old men often play old men's parts well
by merely being themselves.    Of course, real acting
is not just being natural, as some teachers of expression would have their pupils believe.    That idea
is a gross mistake.    Acting is being what you are
not, but giving the impression that what you are
not is what you are.    The professional stage is
flooded with men and women who have little or no
ability for acting, but who appear year in and year
out as leading men or women.    How is it, you ask?
Simple.    They are just natural.    They are themselves on the stage.    They could be no one else if
they tried, for they have no ability as mimics.
Watch the bills of the theatres on Broadway, and
season after season you will see the same "stars"
featured in the same type of part.

But the director should not make the mistake of
keeping a player in a certain kind of part continually
unless that player has no ambition to be an actor.

The whole gamut, from the country sheriff to 'is Lordship, is the ambition of every true actor.

Having chosen the cast carefully, the director and the stage-manager familiarize themselves with the text. The play is "blocked," the setting worked out, the big scenes located, and whatever "cutting" or alterations may be necessary is made.

The first rehearsal, known as the reading rehearsal, is now held. The director gives a brief description of the settings of the play, the location of prominent "props," windows, doors, etc.; and a few remarks about the period and locale.

The players, however, should not be furnished with separate texts, as is sometimes done in amateur theatricals. They should be given a script of the play. This script is a copy of the individual player's lines, his cues, and his positions on the stage. Nothing else should appear on it. It is no longer a question among producers whether or not actors should be provided with scripts or texts. As a rule, the less the player knows about another's part, the better off he is. He then has nothing to confuse him, and it is certainly easier for him to memorize his part.

Of course, this takes the initiative in scene building away from the player, but this is just what is needed.   The director has full sway.

Script sizes are most convenient when cut about 6 x 9.   These sheets should then be firmly bound together.

The director's text should be very complete.   He can either use a printed text or a typewritten one. The latter is much better, especially when the margins are left wide and the spacing is doubled.   This permits room for the writing of notes.   The "business" of each character, diagrams, crossings, tempo, manner of reading lines, etc. will all be indicated on these margins.   Such a script will be prepared in the first few rehearsals.   It is well to have a typewritten copy made of this, with the "business" in red and the notes in parentheses.   Names of characters should be in the center of the page just above the speech.

At the first performance, a reading of the entire

play will be sufficient.   No one is expected to get into his part.   It is merely to give the cast an idea of the play as a whole.   Some directors have each player describe the character he is to impersonate. This is an excellent idea as it helps the player to fix the characterization definitely in his mind.

At the second meeting, which should be held the following day, the real work of rehearsals begins. If it is a full-length play, one act will usually be taken up; if a one-act piece, the entire play.   The director will again carefully describe the setting, mark out the floor with chalk, designate the position of characters and locate "props."

It is imperative that the director should be definite.   He must know every inch of his floor, and know beforehand just where each character should be.   Then he should see that each character is there.

The play will not be taken up at the beginning and followed through.   The big scenes, important entrances and exits, individual character parts, will be taken up and worked over and over again—until they are as near perfect as possible.   Have the blithe ingénue fall into the hero's arms twenty times if necessary, until she can do it as if she meant it. Of course, no director will begin his rehearsal by launching into the big scene. It is much better to begin with the minor ones and coupling-up lines. After five minutes of this the cast is ready for more difficult work.

Rehearsals should never be less than two hours long nor less frequent than three a week. If a play is to be given in a month's time, there should be at least three rehearsals the first week, four the second, five the third, and every day the fourth.

A director once remarked to the author in regard to rehearsal attendance: "I never have trouble with my players getting to rehearsals. They are always there on time and ready for work. The secret is simply this: I work them so hard the first three rehearsals that the lazy ones get interested and the energetic ones enthusiastic. The harder people work on a proposition the more interest they take in it. It's the dilly-dallying that kills."

While the director is preparing the players, his

committee on costuming, scenery and lighting are working out their problems. Consultations with the director should be held by them at least once a week and, if necessary, oftener.

# XII

## ACTING

THE amateur player usually remains an amateur player because he does not know how to become a professional.   He cannot even tell wherein a professional differs from himself.   It is a mistake on the director's part to take the attitude that his players should do certain things because he, the director, wants them to, and without knowing why.   That is well enough for the professional actor, who, having passed through his study period, knows just what the director is driving at.   But with the amateur it is different.   He is probably a very intelligent individual, perhaps more intelligent than the average professional, and for some one to tell him to do something in a certain way because that some one wants it done that way, does not, to say the least, meet his grain.   He will probably do what the director says but he will slouch it.

Some time ago I was watching an autocratic director coach an amateur play in which this very point came up.

"Don't go out the door that way!" he shouted to an actor making an exit.

"Why not?" the actor inquired.

"Because I don't want it done that way," the director replied.  "Do it like this."  And he got up on the stage and showed him how.

The actor probably knew no more about it than before.  He was a mere puppet.

How much better it would have been had the director said: "Hesitate at the door just before going out; that will show Briand's indecision."  The player would at once have caught the idea and felt its effect.

Certainly the amateur player will never learn the meaning of values unless he is told the "why." The director will lose none of his authority in this way, and he will gain in the esteem of his cast.  Of course, the director who works by this method must have his text perfectly.  Perhaps that is why some directors avoid it.  Every movement, every piece of business, every cadence of the voice must have a clear reason for being, and the director should know those reasons.   If a player is to make a pause at the end of a line, if he is to increase the tempo of a passage, if he is to insert a bit of impressive acting, he will do it far more intelligently when shown the

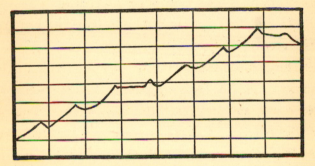

Line of action in the first act of a three-act play showing ascending and falling movements. The cross lines indicate scenes.

reason for doing it in that way, and the next time in a similar place he will do it rememberingly.

No good director will rehearse long stretches of plays until every scene, every movement, every value in that stretch is worked out, memorized and appreciated by the cast.

A play is made up of a chain of scenes and situations, which in most plays increases in intensity until the climax is reached. There are so many steps, each step a scene, and the space between is filled with connecting lines. It ought to be needless to say that every player should understand play construction and know just what a situation is.

The European playwrights in their printed texts indicate every situation as a new scene. Most of the English editions of Ibsen are so divided. For instance, in "A Doll's House," Act II, Scene IV, Nora and Helmer constitute the scene. Scene IV is the attempt of Nora to keep her husband from sending a letter to Krogstad dismissing him. At the end of the scene, Helmer says:

HELMER: It's all the same. You call my reasons petty; then I must be petty too. Petty! Very well then. Now we'll put an end to this once and for all. *Goes to the door into the hall and calls*] Ellen!

NORA: What do you want to do?

HELMER [*searching among his papers*]: To put an end to this whole affair.

The entrance of the servant Ellen, her taking of

the letter and her departure constitute the fifth scene. All that is spoken is:

HELMER [*to Ellen*]: There, take the letter. Give it to a messenger. But see that he takes it at once. The address is on it. Here is the money for him.

Or, from a modern thriller:

Two gold-diggers are seated in a darkened log room in the mountains which is lit by the flickering fire in the hearth. A rickety table is between them on which are two bags of nuggets. A third bag, is dumped on the table and the two men are engaged in counting them. This is one scene, and might have a situation of its own, but the latch of the door lifts noiselessly, the door moves open and a masked figure with a pistol appears. The advent of the third person, with his pistol, his masked face, and his robber air, because he creates a new situation, creates another scene.

"Put 'em up!" the masked man orders.

The two men slide to their feet, their hands in the air. Here the situation is being developed.

"Put 'em down, boys," the would-be robber says,

lowering his gun and removing his mask. "It's me; I just wanta show yer it's not best to keep yer kertain up."

This ends the particular scene. The climax has been reached and the denouement completed.

Now this little picture is merely one of the scenes of the play. Every scene has its situation. The situation may be a minor one; it may be a major one, its climax being the climax of the play, but it is never complete in itself. It depends for its being on a situation or situations preceding it. Its effects may depend on future situations. It is the outcome of other situations, and if a minor one it will, in turn, produce another, which will be more intense. The culmination of this series of steps is the climax. The situations growing out of the climax diminish in intensity. Theoretically the end of the play is not an end at all, for though the situations to the spectator have been relieved for the present, new situations might continue to evolve from the last one in the play, and thus go on forever.

Once the player grasps the idea of scene building

and situation he has taken a long step toward professionalism.

How are scenes built up? A writer on the essentials of play-writing says: "A well constructed play may be fitly compared to a Roman mosaic. It is composed of hundreds of thousands of minute

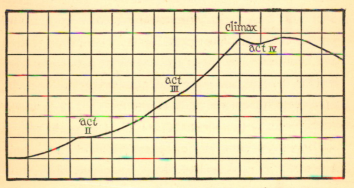

The line of action in a four-act play

pieces, each one of which has its value in creating the general effect, while the absence of any would leave an ugly gap."

Every scene has its beginning, its development, its climax, its denouement and its end. Thus a play is made up of a number of tiny plays, for there are usually fifteen or more scenes to each act. A

flies behind the screen. She has forgotten the fan. The audience knows she has forgotten it, and, what is more, knows that the husband will find it.

Various means are used to place emphasis on the dominant point. The acceleration or retarding of the tempo or flow of words will immediately attract the attention of the audience. The raising or the lowering of the pitch of the voice produces the same effect. The playing of a taper of light on some object on the stage, as in the classic example of "Peter Grimm," the color of a costume, the physical appearance of the actor, are all used to gain emphasis. Emphasis by grouping will be taken up in another chapter.

One point in connection with acting must not be omitted—keeping ahead of the audience. The actor is the moving force; the audience, the movable. To perform his function, then, the actor must know the cause that produces a certain result, and further he must be able to present that cause in order to effect that result. In other words, the actor must see in his mind's eye the result or effect on the audience which a certain movement will produce. The "subconscious mind," "losing one's self" and similar expressions are terms applied to results which are produced by the actor's close study of the part, its effects and characteristics, and his keeping ahead of the audience in applying them. The actor thinks before he acts and the audience, witnessing the action, in turn does its thinking or feeling.

The player must remember that he is not alone on the stage, and that his failure to "play up" to the other actors will not only kill their parts but also make him appear wooden. George Arliss can succeed with a scene that appears almost hopeless at the beginning by his simulation of attention to the actor who is speaking. Every effect of the opposite actor is recorded on Arliss' face or body. A single word will cause him to twitch a muscle, droop his head, brighten his expression in a manner that is absolutely convincing.

Little can be said here about tempo that will be of value to the player. Comedy and light scenes are usually given in quick tempo; sentimental scenes and scenes of deep feeling more slowly. Individual interpretation, governed by the director who sees the play as a whole, will determine these details.

The professional stage will not permit flat or vapid pauses. There are times when no lines are spoken, but these intervals are filled with "business" or with mental activity that does not show vacuity. The player will do well to follow this method. The terror of the pause to the beginner is justified, for it is usually terrifying to the audience; but silences filled with mental activity showing in the actor's expression, or physical "business" inserted appropriately, are appreciated. Pauses should be timed.

It is not my purpose to fill this chapter with obvious "don'ts." There exist already quite enough books on amateur theatricals which contain such lists. The director is the only one who can correct these faults. If the player will keep in mind the following points: that the eyes are the most expressive part of the body; that no movement should be made unless that movement means something and there is a reason for it; that a good actor enunciates clearly, he will present a creditable appearance.

## BIBLIOGRAPHY ON ACTING

BELASCO, DAVID. *The Theatre Through the Stage Door.* Harper, N. Y., 1919.

BLEACKLEY, J. ARTHUR. *The Art of Mimicry.* French, N. Y.

BROADBENT, R. J. *History of Pantomime.* Simpkin, London, 1901.

BURLEIGH, LOUISE. *The Community Theatre.* Little, Brown, Boston, 1917.

CLARK, BARRETT H. *How to Produce Amateur Plays.* Little, Brown, Boston, 1917.

CHENEY, SHELDON. *The Art Theatre.* Knopf, N. Y., 1917.

CALVERT, LOUIS. *The Problem of the Actor.* Holt, N. Y., 1919.

FISKE, MINNIE MADDERN. *Mrs. Fiske: Her Views on Actors, Acting and the Problem of Production.* Century, N. Y., 1917.

HILLIARD, EVELYN, and others. *Amateur and Educational Dramatics.* Macmillan, N. Y., 1918.

HORNBLOW, ARTHUR. *Training for the Stage.* Lippincott, Phil., 1916.

MATTHEWS, BRANDER. *On Acting.* Scribners, N. Y., 1914.

## XIII

## GROUPING

GROUPING or dressing the stage is one of the chief duties of the director. The average beginning player, unless he understands the principles of grouping, can see no reason for the director moving him about from place to place on the stage.

Grouping depends on line and form for the effects, and line and form are the results of spacing and massing of figures. It naturally falls into two types—grouping for mass effects and grouping for individual emphasis. The latter is used most frequently on the indoor stage.

As I have mentioned before in this book, a play should consist of a series of pictures, one moving into another. In forming these pictures, the laws of the pictorial artist are used. The stage picture, then, like the painting, is carefully planned. But grouping, like setting, should be subordinated to the actor and used as an aid to him. Therein lies the difference between stage and pageantry grouping.

The player must not get the idea that grouping is in itself, on the indoor stage, an end. It is merely a method of directing the movements of the actor in order to present the best possible picture.

The grouping of the important scenes of the play is worked out first, and the connective scenes are arranged to lead into the more important ones. In this way the transition appears natural and loses that artificiality so often seen on the amateur stage. For instance, the director wishes to give particular emphasis to a character or wishes to stress a certain bit of acting in a particular scene. He knows that this can be done by giving a portion of the stage to the individual actor, separating him from the others. For instance, he wants his character down stage and the other characters upstage R. The characters in the preceding scene, which will doubt-less be a connective one, will be so arranged that their movement into the required grouping will seem natural and the only thing they should do.

Grouping for emphasis is largely used on the professional stage. The moment two or more people are placed together, they lose their individuality and become a group. The lion roams by himself; sheep go in flocks. To gain emphasis, groups must be separated and the character who has the important point to bring out is moved to a part of the stage where he is alone. He is made conspicuous. The most important part of the stage is down stage centre; then R and L down centre, back centre and R and L back.

The eyes of the audience can focus only on one object at one time. A scene where two men stand close together quarreling does not "get over." The audience sees them as a group. Place a table between them and observe the difference. They become individuals and the attention of the audience can shift from one to the other as each man speaks.

Another physical means of gaining emphasis is to bring the players down stage, grouping them in a triangular shape with the emphatic character at the apex. Attention is at once directed to him. Striking entrances and exits and emphasis of balance are also used.

The sooner the player realizes that every mosaic is a picture, the sooner the director will be freed from the aimless and nervous moving about of beginners. Players should not get the idea that they are forming a set of tableaux. This will make them artificial. They must learn the necessity of standing and moving about under definite regulations to produce certain effects, and they must realize that at all times the stage must be balanced.

Greek and Shakespearean plays, modern poetical drama, phantasies and folk plays readily lend themselves to pictorial grouping, and many of them may be staged with the technique of pageantry.

### BIBLIOGRAPHY ON GROUPING

BEEGLE, MARY PORTER and CRAWFORD, JACK RANDALL. *Community Drama and Pageantry*. Yale University Press, 1916.

CHUBB, PERCIVAL, and others. *Festivals and plays in Schools and Elsewhere*. Harper, N. Y., 1912.

CLARK, BARRETT H. *How to Produce Amateur Plays*. Little, Brown, Boston, 1917

FROHMAN, DANIEL. *Memories of a Manager.* Double-day, Garden City, 1911.

KROWS, ARTHUR EDWIN. *Play Production in America.* Holt, N. Y., 1916.

TAYLOR, EMERSON. *Practical Stage Directing for Amateurs.* Dutton, N. Y., 1916.

## XIV

## COLOR

The most subtle of all stage devices is color. Modern stage art has learned this and, as a result, color is one of the principal elements of a production. Color, through lighting, was touched upon in the chapter on Lighting. A few suggestions will be made here as to pigment coloring.

Briefly, for the player, there are two kinds of color—"cold" and "warm." Green, blue and purple, nature's chief robes, represent the cold colors; reds, oranges and yellows, the warm. From a natural standpoint, the grouping is correct. The sky, the water, the woods, the purple of the dawn and the summit of the hills are cold—uninviting. They seem distant, unfriendly. On the other hand, the glowing sunset, the yellow moon coming up through the trees, the tinted forest in the Fall, all seem filled with warmth—and all are fleeting. They cast a spell for a moment and are gone.   Nature's colors are mostly cold.

Just so the cold colors should predominate on the stage; the warm to be used in contrast and to produce emotion.

Colors are used visually for decorative and symbolical purposes.   A pure white costume may be used for contrast with the setting; it may also signify the purity of the wearer.

For decorative purposes, complementary, contrasting and luminous colors are used.   A background of green will give a touch of red a brilliant effect; or a background of blue will act in the same way with yellow.   Oftentimes color modulations of varying shades are used for an entire scene.   The player must remember, however, that he is working by artificial illumination with pigment and light and that colors appear under a very different form in the sunlight.   Experimentation on the model stage with an understanding of the primary and secondary colors, their complements and their shades is the best recourse.

The conventional use of symbolical colors is still

prevalent on the stage.   In light, scenery and costume, white stands for purity and innocence.   Red
still retains its signification of faithful love and
passionate zeal; yellow indicates jealousy and de-
ceit; green, youth and springtime; the devil and
his friends are still black; royalty yet wears purple,
and heaven with all its promise is still blue.

The emotional side of color must not be ignored.
Cold colors, greens, blues and purples, produce seriousness in the audience; warm colors, reds, oranges
and yellows reduced to a very low tone, produce an
excited seriousness and when raised continue to ex-
cite the emotions in a greater degree.   Very high
tones of the cold colors act in the same way.   The
player will remember that color, like music, is subtle in its power of exciting the emotions.

Unless there is a particular reason for contrast,
the dividing line of colors should not be marked.
It is better to let one hue run into another.   Producers, as a general rule, place the softer and more
natural colors in the background of the stage and
the more vivid in the front.

The producer need not strive at scientific correctness of color.   Approximation will serve.   If his stage is equipped with amber, blue and white lights, green floods and spots, he can approximate any color.

In the Community Playhouse, one member at least on each of the committees on Lighting and Costuming should have a working knowledge of pigment and light colors.   With the assistance of the director and an electrician, little trouble should be experienced in obtaining the desired results.

The following table, referring to colored lights on colored material, will be of benefit to the student:

### THE WARM COLORS

*Red light* on pigment of

Yellow, gives orange; dark green, yellow-black; light green, red-gray; blue, violet; violet, deep purple; black, purplish black; orange, red-orange; red, deep red.

*Orange light* on pigment of

Black, gives deep brown; red, scarlet; yellow, yellow-orange; light green, rusty green; dark green, yellow-green; light blue, orange gray; dark blue, dull gray; indigo, dark brown; violet, red-brown.

*Yellow light* on pigment of

Black, gives yellow-olive; red, orange; orange, yellow-orange; green, yellow-green; light blue, yellow-green; dark blue, green slate; indigo, orange-yellow; violet, yellow-brown.

## THE COLD COLORS

*Green light* on pigment of

Black, gives green-brown; red, brown; orange, faint yellow with green tinge; yellow, brilliant yellow-green; blue, intense green; indigo, dull green; violet, bluish green-brown.

*Blue light* on pigment of

Yellow, gives green; green, blue-green; indigo, deep blue-indigo; violet, dark blue-violet; black, blue-black; orange, brown with a tint of yellow; red, violet.

*Violet light* on pigment of

Black, gives black with a faint violet tinge; red, red-violet-purple; orange, light red; yellow, brown with pale tint of red; green, light purple; blue, clear blue-violet; indigo, deep indigo-violet.

The mixing of colors is really not a difficult task once the principles are understood.

The following table will give an idea of the mixing of pigments.

The primary colors are: red, yellow, blue.

The secondary colors result from a mixture of a certain number of parts of the primary colors.

| RED | YELLOW | BLUE | | |
|---|---|---|---|---|
| 2 parts | 2 parts | 0 parts | gives orange | } secondary colors |
| 0 " | 2 " | 2 " | " green | |
| 2 " | 0 " | 2 " | " violet | |

Tertiary colors result from a mixture of the primaries in the following proportions:

| RED | YELLOW | BLUE | | | |
|---|---|---|---|---|---|
| 3 | 0 | 1 | gives | violet red | } Tertiary colors |
| 3 | 1 | 0 | " | red orange | |
| 1 | 3 | 0 | " | orange yellow | |
| 0 | 3 | 1 | " | yellow green | |
| 0 | 1 | 3 | " | greenish blue | |
| 1 | 0 | 3 | " | blue violet | |

An equal mixture of the three primaries will give neutral gray.

The Community Playhouse worker will be compelled to learn through experience many things about both light and pigment color. He will find that his goal will never be reached, that his utmost in experimentation will reward him but lightly, and that he can lay down few if any rules which will work twice under what appear to be the same conditions. Let him keep before him the fact, however, that the human eye is a very sensitive organ, that its possibilities of reception are unlimited and that it is one of the chief channels to the emotions of his audience.

## BIBLIOGRAPHY ON COLOR

BEEGLE, MARY PORTER and CRAWFORD, JACK RANDALL. *Community Drama and Pageantry*. Yale University Press, 1916.

CHENEY, SHELDON. *The Art Theatre*. Knopf, N. Y., 1917.

CHREVREUL, MICHAEL EUGENE. *Principles of Harmony and Contrasts of Color*. Macmillan, N. Y., 1904.

CHUBB, PERCIVAL, and others. *Festivals and plays in Schools and Elsewhere*. Harper, N. Y., 1912.

CHURCH, ARTHUR HERBERT. *Color: Elementary Manual*. Cassell, N. Y., 1908.

FERREE, CLARENCE ERROLL, and others. *Color Symposium*. Illuminating Engineering Society, N. Y., 1917.

HATT, JOSEPH ARTHUR HENRY. Colorist—*Practical Information for Artists and Workers and Designers in Colors*. 2nd Ed. Van Nostrand, N. Y., 1913.

HURST, GEORGE HENRY. *A Handbook of the Theory of Color*. 2nd Ed. Van Nostrand, N. Y., 1916.

IRWIN, BEATRICE. *New Science of Color*. Unwin, London, 1915.

KROWS, ARTHUR EDWIN. *Play Production in America*. Holt, N. Y., 1916.

LUCKIESH, MARION. *Color and Its Application*. Van Nostrand, N. Y., 1915.

MODERWELL, HIRAM KELLY. *The Theatre of To-day*. Lane, N. Y., 1914.

# XV

## COSTUMES

UPON the costumes committee falls the responsibility of designing and providing the players with costumes. The ability of this committee will decide to a marked degree the amateurishness or success of the performance, for costuming is one of the principal elements of a production. Not only must this committee understand designing, but if the playhouse is to be run economically it must have a knowledge of dyeing, stencilling, painting, gilding, embroidering, cutting, fitting, sewing and draping and, if there is no committee on properties, molding.

Four points should be observed by the committee in making costumes: period, appropriateness, color and fit.

Every costume should be designed for a certain period. If a play is set in the seventeenth century, then every man, woman and child in the play will dress as men, women and children of the seventeenth century dressed. Every visible article of clothing will belong to that period. If the play calls for a twentieth century setting and costumes, then the characters will appear in twentieth century clothing. In phantasies, poetical and other plays, not set in any definite period, the costumes will be designed for pictorial effectiveness, suitability to the character and to the play and general impression.

The color of the costume will harmonize with the color of the setting. Principles of harmony of color will have to be observed. The clashing of hues and colors that give undue prominence will both be avoided. Gay-spirited characters will not wear sombre hues nor vice versa. Neither will red and orange, brown and tan, yellow and gold and other clashing shades be thrown together.

The making of costumes in the laboratory of the Community Playhouse has done much to get rid of the laughable monstrosities of amateur theatricals when costumes are rented. For a few dollars the artist designer, the skillful craftsmen of the players' group, can turn out a costume that is almost perfect.

Especially does this apply to costumes for the female members. Dress suits for men and similar costumes present a certain difficulty. These must be rented if the actors do not possess their own, and nothing is more disturbing to a player's peace of mind than to know that his sleeves are too short or his trousers too big, or that his shoes are modern while the rest of his costume is of another period. "He knows he's correct and he shows it" reads the modern clothing advertisement. It reads rightly. No player should go on the stage unless he feels that every stitch of clothing on him is just right—correct in every way. This is the duty of the costume committee, and they should feel that if some ill-attired Romeo forgets his lines in the midst of his passion it is probably due to his having become conscious of the fit of his waistcoat.

Costumes made by the committee for the group need not be of expensive material. Many of the cheaper grades look just as well under artificial light. Canton flannel resembles velvet on the stage and will hang better. Cambric looks like silk, and other cheap materials simulate more expensive cloth.

Always design costumes first, choosing colors that will fit in with the color scheme of the setting. The designing artist usually draws his designs in silhouette in order to obtain the form effect.

The centuries are growing misty. Only a few archæologists care whether the costume of a Hamlet is of the eleventh or the thirteenth century, provided it conveys the idea of belonging to a century sufficiently far back. We do care, however, if half his costume belongs to the twelfth century and the remainder to the twentieth.

Details of costumes are lost on the stage; it is the general effect that counts.

### BIBLIOGRAPHY ON COSTUME

ABRAHAM, ETHEL BEATRICE. *Greek Dress*. Murray, London, 1908.

ARIA, MRS. E. *Costume, Fanciful, Historical and Theatrical*. Macmillan, N. Y., 1906.

ASHODOON, MRS. C. H. *British Costume*. Stokes, N. Y., 1910.

BARFIELD, T. C. *Longman's Historical Illustrations*. Longmans, N. Y., 1911.

BEEGLE, MARY PORTER and CRAWFORD, JACK RANDALL. *Community Drama and Pageantry*. Yale University Press, 1916.

BOWER, CYRIL. *Stage Costume*. French, N. Y., 1910.

CALTHORP, DION CLAYTON. *English Costume*. Black, N. Y., 1906.

CHENEY, SHELDON. *The Art Theatre*. Knopf, N. Y., 1917.

CLARK, BARRETT H. *How to Produce Amateur Plays*. Little, Brown, Boston, 1917.

DEMMIN AUGUSTE. *Illustrated History of Arms and Armor*. Macmillan, N. Y.

EARLE, ALICE MORSE. *Costume in Colonial Times*. Scribners, N. Y., 1912.

EARLE, ALICE MORSE. *Two Centuries of Costume in America*. New Edition, Macmillan, N. Y., 1910.

EVANS, MARIA MILLINGTON. *Chapters on Greek Dress*. Macmillan, N. Y., 1893.

FAIRCHILD, F. W. *Costume in England*. Beel, London, 1893.

GUPTILL, MRS. ELIZABETH FRANCES and WORMWOOD, EDYTH M. *Amateur's Costume Nook*. Edridge Entertainment House, 1917.

HOLT, ARDERN. *Fancy Dress Described*. 6th Ed. Longmans, London, 1915.

RHEAD, G. WOOLISCROFT. *Chats on Costume*. Stokes, N. Y., 1906.

TRAPHAGEN, ETHEL H. *Costume Design and Illustrations*. Wiley, N. Y., 1918.

# XVI

## CONCLUSION

The Little Theatre in some form has come to stay. No one doubts this who has followed the movement since its beginning in 1911. Not only has it gathered force since that year, but it has ceased to be suspected as it was in its youth. When Maurice Browne went to Chicago and announced to the public his intention of establishing a miniature theatre seating less than a hundred people, he was at once proclaimed a faddist.

To-day there are more than seventy little theatres in the United States. Interest in them is spreading from one end of the country to the other. Every year sees the birth of new ones. To be sure, they are not all of the same type, nor are all doing the same quality of work. Some are groups of artists working for their own advancement; members of others are working for the pleasure of working; some fill a social need, some an educational. Moreover, there are hundreds of clubs and societies throughout the country which, owing to the influence of the little theatre, are doing creditable work in dramatics.

I have preferred to call the little theatre outlined in this book a Community Playhouse, because whatever else this type of theatre performs it is a means whereby the community can express itself. And this type is one of the most enduring. Most of the theatres of the West and Middle West are of this variety and to the Middle West belongs the inception of the movement. Talented groups like the Washington Square Players and the Provincetown Players will spring into existence from time to time and demand recognition, but it is interesting to note that the former group, while not having a federated audience, relied on patrons to some extent; and that, even in spite of this and their own excellent work, they were compelled to disband.

The Community Playhouse is built to fill a need. Like any other institution, a theatre without a purpose is of no use to humanity. There is no period in the world's history that boasts of a great dramatic renaissance founded on the principle "the theatre for the theatre's sake." There is always a small minority in every period—usually made up of dilettanti—who, however, choose such phrases and proceed to act upon them. They draw themselves off into little cliques, assume a superior air, and label all who do not agree with them coarse business men. We are at present in this country annoyed by a few such groups, but their influence is not likely to prove very detrimental. There is no doubt that the "superior" theatre will reach a certain audience. But should the public that patronizes it label other publics as course and ignorant? I appreciate an art gallery (as well as an Art Theatre) but the business man who lives just across the street from me cannot tell the difference between a Fra Filippo Lippi and a Fra Angelico, nor does he care whether or not either of these artists ever drew a breath or a fresco. He will laugh by the hour with a Rip Van Winkle or cry with a Music Master and he can tell the history of the man who draws Polly and Her Pals. He can even tell you his technical faults. But he will be bored to the bone if he is compelled to sit through a performance of a so-called "artistic" group.

The fact I want to bring out is that the "superior" theatre or group or any other kind can no more satisfy all the audiences of the country than can the commercial theatre. It appeals to a limited class and there is no need to try to force it on the whole.

What is the future of the Community Playhouse in this country? Will it be like the Prairie Playhouse at Galesburg, Illinois—from gin to Galsworthy and from Galsworthy to groceries? I think not. Though there may be failures, due to the unnaturalness of the times, the inopportune establishment of a theatre, highbrowism and other causes, the Community Playhouse has come to stay. And it has come to stay because it has a purpose—better plays.

Certainly I do not mean by "better plays" the choice of a certain group or clique, but a higher standard, whenever that is possible, in acting, staging and writing for each public. Condemn the commercial theatre and its branches as we may, we cannot get away from the fact that the best acting in the Little Theatres has never been consistently equal to the best acting or even, in most cases, to the average acting, on the commercial stage. What do we need most? Better acting in the Little Theatres.

On the other hand, staging in the insurgent theatres has, until recently, been far superior to that of the commercial theatres. The leaders in the new stagecraft have done a great deal of experimenting, much of it good, much of it foolish and bad, and the commercial theatres, being commercial and therefore far-sighted, bided their time. At the propitious moment, having kept their eyes on the current, the men of business merely chartered the sturdiest leaders of the new stagecraft and appropriated their cargo.

But the future of the Little Theatre lies neither in staging nor in acting, but rather in the field—a field which many of them have thus far ignored—of training and developing the American playwright. As long as American Little Theatres specialize in Shaw, Ibsen, Dunsany, Maeterlinck and other foreign dramatists, they are missing their

great opportunity. We Americans will not bend
the knee commercially to the Old World, but in art
we grovel in the dust. Why? Simply because we
are drilled that way. An American playwright
writes a clever little skit and all the would-be critics
and foreign-fed artists in the country exclaim:
"Clever! But look at Herr So-and-So in compari-
son!" What we need is an Americanization of art
as well as citizenship. European plays should no
more dominate in our stage than should European
manners and customs dominate in our homes. Until we produce a group of American playwrights
who give us plays interpreting American life and
institutions truthfully, we will be a nation of imi-
tators. To produce that group we must provide an
avenue for them. Suppose we are a nation with a
vaudeville taste; then let us develop vaudeville to
a perfect art, and not feed ourselves on half-baked
productions of exotic composition.

Personally, I do not think that there should be any
great quarrel between the commercial and the little
theatre. The Little Theatre should be a training
school for the larger theatre just as the college or

university is a training school for the business or professional world. Here the writer, the actor, the stage man may learn the fundamentals of his art and his ability as a workman will find him his future place. As long as the commercial theatres and the Little Theatres of this country keep one goal in mind—the development of an American drama—so long will we make progress artistically.

"Better plays" does not mean the importation of foreign workmanship. It means the Americanization of the American stage and the development in all its branches of an American dramatic art. The Community Playhouse is a laboratory for this development. Upon it rests the burden of providing some of the men and women to carry on this work. If it is to have a future, and most of us believe it has, its roots must be firmly and unquestionably planted in American soil. Whatever kind of public any playhouse must satisfy—imaginative or materialistic, lovers of poetry, realism, farce or melodrama, that playhouse, to survive, must give the public the best of its type which America produces.

Then and not until then will we, in dramatic art, become a creative people.

GENERAL BIBLIOGRAPHY

*Album du Vieux Colombier*, par Fauconnet.  Adart, N. Y., 1918.

BAKSHY, ALEKSANDR.  *The Path of the Modern Russian Stage*.  Luce, Boston, 1918.

BARKER, HARLEY GRANVILLE.  *The Exemplary Theatre*. Little, Brown, Boston, 1922.

BEEGLE, MARY PORTER and CRAWFORD, JACK RANDALL. *Community Drama and Pageantry*.  Yale University Press, 1916.

BURLEIGH, LOUISE.  *The Community Theatre*.  Little, Brown, Boston, 1917.

CHENEY, SHELDON.  *The Art Theatre*.  Knopf, N. Y., 1917.

CHENEY, SHELDON.  *The New Movement in the Theater*. Kennerley, N. Y., 1914.

CHENEY, SHELDON.  *The Open-air Theatre*.  Kennerley, N. Y., 1918.

CLARK, BARRETT H.  *How to Produce Amateur Plays*. Little, Brown, Boston, 1917.

DICKINSON, THOMAS H.  *The Insurgent Theatre*. Huebsch, N. Y., 1917.

FRANK, WALDO.  *Art of the Vieux Colombier*.  La Nouvelle Revue Française, Paris.  Columbia Theatre, 65 W. 35th St., N. Y., 1918.

GORDON, EDGAR BERNARD. *Community Music and Drama.* University of Wisconsin Bulletin Ser. No. 843, General Ser. No. 638.

HAMILTON, CLAYTON. *Studies in Stagecraft.* Holt, N. Y., 1914.

HOWE, P. P. *The Repertory Theatre.* Kennerley, N. Y., 1914.

MacGOWAN, KENNETH, and JONES, ROBERT EDMOND. *Continental Stagecraft.* Harcourt, Brace, N. Y., 1922.

MacGOWAN, KENNETH. *The Theatre of To-morrow.* Boni & Liveright, 1922.

MACKAY, CONSTANCE D'ARCY. *The Little Theatre in the United States.* Holt, N. Y., 1917.

MacKAYE, PERCY. *Community Drama.* Houghton, Boston, 1917.

MacKAYE, PERCY. *The Civic Theatre.* Kennerley, N. Y., 1909.

MITCHELL, ROY. *Shakespeare for Community Players.* Dutton, N. Y., 1919.

MODERWELL, HIRAM KELLY. *The Theatre of To-day.* Lane, N. Y., 1914.

NATHAN, GEORGE JEAN. *Mr. George Jean Nathan Presents.* Knopf, N. Y., 1917.

PHELPS, WILLIAM LYON. *The Twentieth Century Theatre.* Macmillan, N. Y., 1918.

## BIBLIOGRAPHY OF TECHNIQUE

ANDREWS, CHARLTON. *Technique of Playwriting.* Home Correspondence School, Springfield, Mass., 1915.

ARCHER, WILLIAM. *Playmaking: A Manual of Crafts-manship*. Small, Maynard, Boston, 1912.

BAKER, GEORGE PRICE. *The Technique of the Drama*. Houghton, Boston, 1915.

BAKER, GEORGE PRICE. *The Dramatic Technique*. Houghton, Boston, 1919.

BURTON, RICHARD. *How to See a Play*. Macmillan, N. Y., 1914.

CANNON, FANNY. *Writing and Selling a Play*. Holt, N. Y., 1915.

HAMILTON, CLAYTON. *Theory of the Theatre*. Holt, N. Y., 1910.

HOPKINS, ARTHUR. *How's Your Second Act?* Goodman, N. Y., 1918.

LEWIS, B. ROLAND. *The Technique of the One-Act Play*. Luce, Boston, 1918.

PRICE, W. T. *Technique of the Drama*. Brentano, N. Y., 1909.

### BIBLIOGRAPHY OF MAKE-UP

CLARK, BARRETT H. *How to Produce Amateur Plays*. Little, Brown, Boston, 1917.

MORTON, CAVEN. *The Art of Theatrical Make-Up*. Macmillan, N. Y., 1909.

TAYLOR, EMERSON. *Practical Stage Directing for Amateurs*. Dutton, N. Y., 1916.

### PLAY LISTS

*Actable One-Act Plays*. Chicago Public Library, 1916. One of the best lists published up to that date. Gives comment on play, number of characters and settings.

CHENEY, SHELDON. *The Art Theatre.* Knopf, 1917. Gives lists of plays produced at the Arts and Crafts Theatre, Detroit.

CLAPP, JOHN MANTEL. *Plays for Amateurs.* Drama League of America, Chicago, 1915.

DICKINSON, THOMAS H. *The Insurgent Theatre.* Huebsch, N. Y., 1917. Contains a list of plays that had been produced in Little Theatres up to that date. Excellent reference for new groups.

*Dramas and Plays.* Compiled by J. Bentley Mulford, F. W. Faxon Company, Boston, 1922. An index to dramatic compositions published in the United States in 1921. Pamphlet form.

DRUMMOND, A. M. *Fifty One-Act Plays.* Quarterly Journal of Public Speaking, Vol. I, p. 234, 1915.

*Plays for Amateurs.* A selective list of one-act and longer plays prepared by the Little Theatre department of the Drama League of New York. H. W. Wilson Company, N. Y., 1921.

*Plays for Children.* A selective list. Compiled for the Drama League of New York by Kate Oglebay. H. W. Wilson Company, N. Y., 1922.

*Plays for Children.* An annotated index compiled by Alice I. Hazeltine. American Library Association, Chicago, 1921.

*Selected List of Christmas Plays.* Drama League Calendar, Nov. 15, 1918. New York.

*Selected List of Patriotic Plays and Pageants Suitable for Amateurs.*  Drama League Calendar, Oct. 1, 1918. New York.

SHAY, FRANK.  *The Plays and Books of the Little Theatre.*  Theatre Arts Crafts Exchange, New York, 1919.